How To...

INCLUDES ONLINE VIDEO LESSONS WITH DEMONSTRATIONS OF ALL THE PLAYING EXAMPLES IN THE BOOK

STRUM CHORDS ON GUITAR

T0066177

A Step-by-Step
Beginner's Guide
for Acoustic or
Electric Guitar

by Burgess Speed

To access video visit:
www.halleonard.com/mylibrary

Enter Code
2844-4436-1447-1450

Video Performer: Chad Johnson

ISBN 978-1-4950-5477-8

HAL•LEONARD®

7777 W. BLUEMOUND RD. P.O. BOX 13819 MILWAUKEE, WI 53213

In Australia Contact:
Hal Leonard Australia Pty. Ltd.
4 Lentara Court
Cheltenham, Victoria, 3192 Australia
Email: ausadmin@halleonard.com.au

Visit Hal Leonard Online at
www.halleonard.com

CONTENTS

INTRODUCTION ▶

Everyone should know how to strum chords on the guitar. What greater form of relaxation is there than sitting somewhere, alone or with some friends, and strumming some tunes? It's not hard; it just takes a little time and the desire to make music. Learning your first chords is easy with *How to Strum Chords on Guitar* because it walks you through simple chord fingerings on three strings first—then four strings, five strings, and finally all six strings. You will build up your right-hand strumming technique as your fretting hand forms increasingly challenging chords. You will learn various musical styles and techniques through short examples and familiar songs. Blues, rock, country, funk, and folk—it's all here and at your fingertips.

Decide right now to dedicate at least 15 minutes a day to learning how to strum chords on the guitar, and you will have a never-ending source of satisfaction and enjoyment. It's helpful if you have some musical experience to start, but it's not necessary. If you have any question about how something should sound, be sure to check out the accompanying video.

ABOUT THE VIDEO

Each chapter in the book includes a full video lesson, so you can see and hear the material being taught. To access all of the videos that accompany this book, simply go to **www.halleonard.com/mylibrary** and enter the code found on page 1. The music examples that include video are marked with an icon throughout the book, and the timecode listed with each icon tells you exactly where on the video the example is performed.

THE STRUMMING HAND

Check out the picture below for the correct way to hold the guitar. Notice where the strumming arm rests on the guitar's body. To start, strum over the sound hole, as this will produce the fullest, loudest sound. Hold your pick between the thumb and index finger (as seen in the picture below). Do not hold it too tightly, as this will make your strumming sound stiff and abrasive. When strumming down, the tip of the pick should point upward; when strumming up, the tip of the pick should point downward. The wrist should make a gentle figure-8 when alternating between downstrokes and upstrokes. Strum lightly—do not dig the pick into the strings, as this will also produce an unpleasant sound. (Note: There will be more strumming instructions in the chapters to come.)

How to hold a guitar

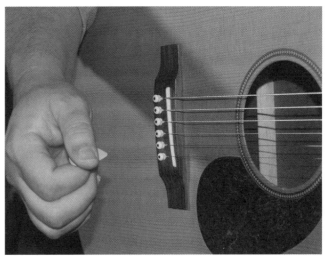

How to hold a pick

Point pick up for downstrokes

Point pick down for upstrokes

A NOTE ABOUT PICKS

Guitar picks come in various thicknesses: extra light, light, medium, heavy, and extra heavy. For strumming, a pick of medium thickness is advised at first, as a light pick may seem too flimsy and a heavy pick will not have any "give," making it harder to strum smoothly. More about picks can be found on page 39 (Tonal Considerations).

Although this book is intended for players who use guitar picks, you could also use your thumb for downstrokes and the index finger for upstrokes. The flesh of the fingers has a warm sound, but it lacks the precision, volume, and potential speed of a pick.

BASIC FRETTING-HAND TECHNIQUE

For classical guitar technique, it's necessary to position the thumb in the middle of the back of the guitar neck. When strumming chords, this is not necessary. In fact, it's often not helpful. Grip the neck as shown in the photo below, with the thumb poking out over the top of the fretboard. You should be able to pick the guitar up with this grip. The only part of your palm that should make contact with the back of the neck is the section in a direct line between the thumb and index finger—nowhere else. The fretting-hand fingers should curl in toward the strings in order to press, or fret, the strings with the fingertips (no flat fingers!). In addition, the finger should be positioned just to the left of the fret wire (just to the right for left-handed guitarists). Check out the following photos.

Standard grip for fretting chords (front view)

Do not touch the neck with any part of the palm except the section between the thumb and index finger (side view)

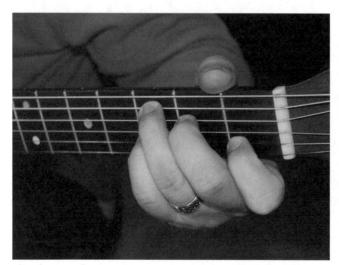

Curl your fingers to press strings with fingertips

Press the strings just to the left of the fret wire

HOW TO READ CHORD DIAGRAMS, RHYTHMIC NOTATION, AND TABLATURE (TAB)

CHORD DIAGRAMS

Chords can be depicted with *chord diagrams*, which are vertical representations of the fretboard showing the strings, frets, and notes to play. Check out the diagram to the right with its components labeled.

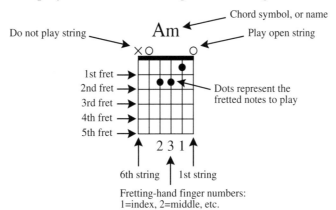

RHYTHMIC NOTATION

Most of this book uses *rhythmic notation* to communicate the strum patterns. Below, you will see the various note values (durations) and how to count them. Each note represents a chord strum.

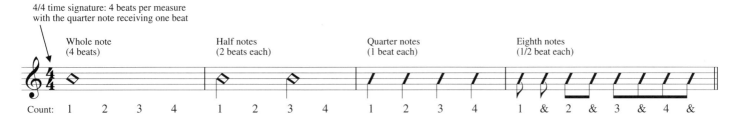

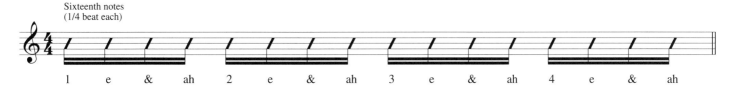

TABLATURE (TAB)

Tablature, also known as *tab*, is another form of notation used in this book. The tab staff has six horizontal lines, each indicating a guitar string. Numbers are used to show which fret to play on which string. In some tab, stems and beams are included to indicate note value, and circled numbers under the staff signify fretting-hand fingers. This is the system used in this book.

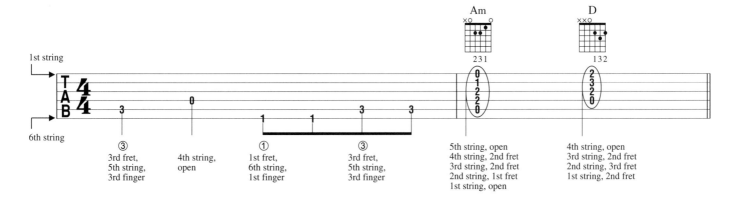

CHAPTER 1

CHORDS ON THE TOP THREE STRINGS

A *chord* consists of three or more notes played at the same time. The most basic type of chord is a *triad*, or three-note chord, which can be played conveniently on three strings (one note for each string). This chapter features chords on the top three strings (strings 1–3, the strings closest to the floor when holding the guitar), so let's begin by getting used to strumming these strings.

Don't worry about fretting any notes or keeping time yet—just get used to the mechanics of this strum. Start with your pick just above the third string and then sweep it downward through and just past the first string. Then bring the pick back to starting position and strum again. Remember, the pick should be angled with the tip pointing upward to avoid any resistance against the strings. With the correct angle, it bounces lightly from string to string. Repeat this process until you are comfortable with the mechanics of the strum.

The chord you just played, strings 1–3 open, is an E minor chord. The chord symbol used to represent this chord in written music is "Em."

TYPES OF CHORDS

For most of this book, we will be using four types of chords: major, minor, major seventh, and dominant seventh. Below is a chart showing the type of chord, its general tonal quality, its chord suffix, and an example chord symbol in C.

Type	Tonal Quality	Suffix	Example
Major	upbeat or happy	No suffix	C
Minor	Introspective or sad	m	Cm
Major seventh	Pleasant or bright	maj7	Cmaj7
Dominant seventh	Bluesy or unstable ("wants" to resolve to another chord)	7	C7

Now, let's play the Em chord in time. We will count "1, 2, 3, 4; 1, 2, 3, 4" and strum downward on each beat. In addition, tap your foot, bringing it down on each count. Remember to keep a steady, consistent rhythm, focusing on nice even strums. Let's give it a try.

⊓ = Downstroke, strum downward

EXAMPLE 1 • 0:49

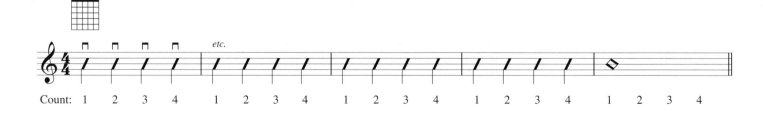

Now, let's put our third finger on the third fret of string 1. This produces a G chord. Practice going back and forth between Em and G by placing and removing your third finger. Don't worry about the time at first. Once you feel comfortable with the change, try switching between the chords in rhythm, strumming four beats for each chord as in Example 2.

EXAMPLE 2 • 1:38

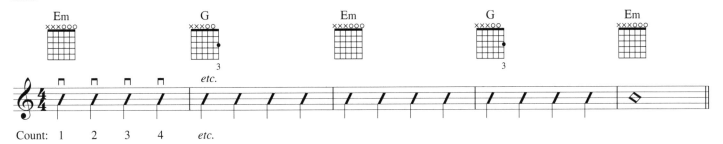

If we use our second finger to press the second fret of string 1, we get G major 7th, or Gmaj7. Practice changing between these two chords by switching back and forth between your third and second fingers and strumming each time. Once you have that down, try it in rhythm.

EXAMPLE 3 • 2:24

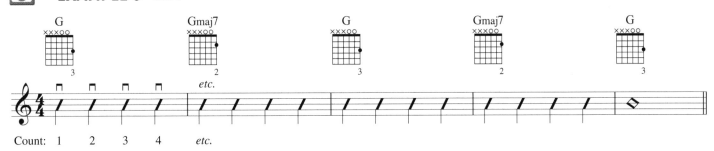

Placing our first finger on the first fret of string 1 gives us G7. Before trying the next example, practice switching between Gmaj7 and G7 (second finger to first finger), the new change introduced in this example. Now, try Example 4.

EXAMPLE 4 • 3:14

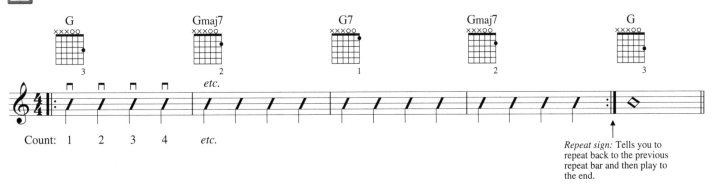

Repeat sign: Tells you to repeat back to the previous repeat bar and then play to the end.

Example 5 features our first chord with a finger fretting the second string. Placing your first finger on the first fret of string 2 gives us a C chord. Practice going back and forth between G7 and C and then play through Example 5. This is really starting to sound like music now, right? In fact, many songs use chord progressions similar to this, including "Something" by the Beatles.

EXAMPLE 5 · 4:19

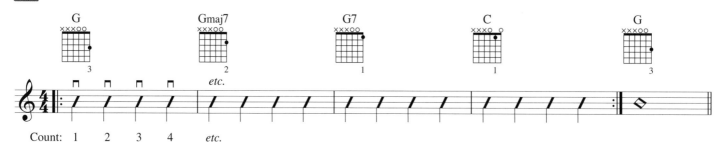

Put your first finger in position for a C chord and then add your second finger to the second fret of string 3. This fingering (which is our first two-finger chord) creates an Am chord. Practice going back and forth between the two chords and then try the example below.

EXAMPLE 6 · 5:30

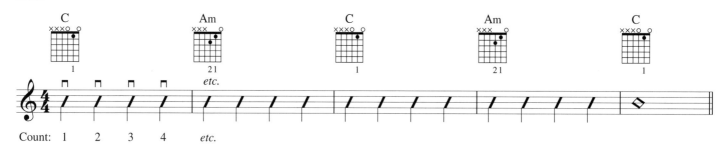

Here is another example featuring Am.

EXAMPLE 7 · 6:00

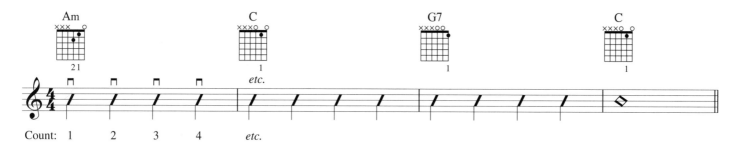

Example 8 features a new chord, E, with the first finger on the first fret of string 3. This is also our first example where we are changing between chords within a measure. In measure 4, we play Am on beats 1–2 and E on beats 3–4. Practice switching between these two chords before trying this example in time. (Note: To develop a good sense of time, practice with a metronome or other time-keeping device. Start off slowly and then increase the speed, or *tempo*, as you become more accustomed to the chord changes.)

EXAMPLE 8 · 6:43

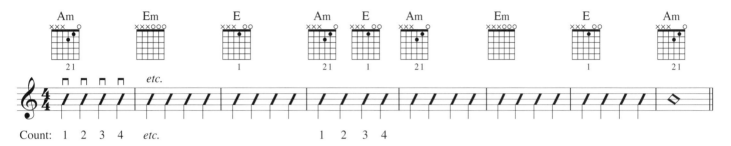

Let's put Examples 5 and 8 together for the next exercise. You should be used to all of these chord changes now, but double check them before trying this example in rhythm.

EXAMPLE 9 · 7:24

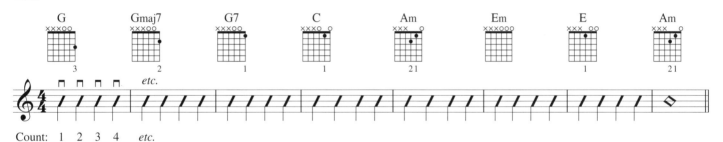

SOME NOTES ON PRACTICING

- **Always practice mechanics first:** Practice making tricky switches between chords before you play the example as a whole. Isolate any trouble spots and work on the physical requirements of the music before trying to play it in time.

- **Repetition is key:** Practice the challenging parts over and over again until they are comfortable.

- **When attempting to play an example in rhythm, start off slowly and gradually build up speed** as your hands become more accustomed to what is required of them.

- **Use a metronome:** As mentioned on the previous page, a metronome, or other time-keeping device (such as a mobile app), will help you develop a great sense of time. You can start slowly and increase the tempo in a steady, consistent, and quantifiable manner.

- **Have patience:** If you consistently practice for at least 15 minutes a day for at least 5 days a week, you will make steady and noticeable progress.

- **Lastly, enjoy yourself:** Learning and playing an instrument is great for the mind, body, and soul!

Let's look at a couple of longer examples now.

Next up is a blues tune. Later in this book, we'll talk more about what makes a blues progression, but for now, we can say that it is 12 measures (or *bars*) long and features three different chords. "Three-String Blues" includes a new chord, D7 (see right). The change from G to D7 involves sliding your third finger down to the second fret and then placing your first and second fingers in their correct positions. This change may take some practice. Just go back and forth between those two chords until you are comfortable with the transition.

THREE-STRING BLUES

8:28

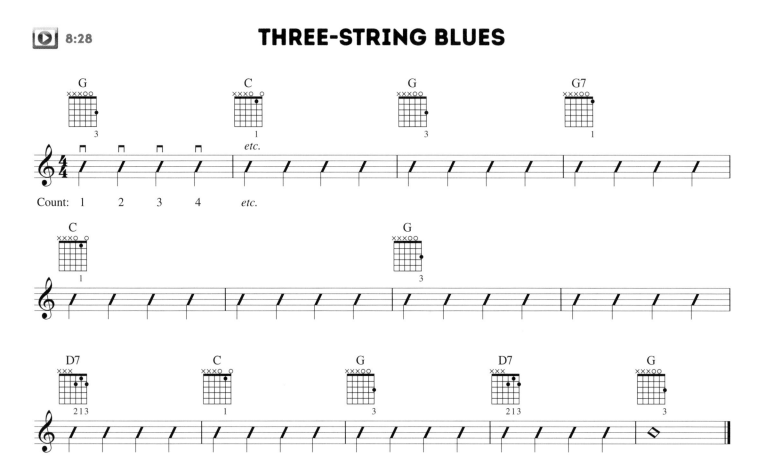

The next example is a lot of fun to play. It's in the style of the Johnny Rivers tune "Secret Agent Man," which was the theme song for *Secret Agent*, a short-lived but popular 1960s television show.

There are a couple of new chords here: A7 and B7 (see chord diagrams). A7 appears in a simple sequence (Am–C–A7–C), in which only the note on the second string changes—from the open string to the first fret to the second fret and back to the first fret. Check out the first two measures of "Undercover" and practice this over and over. You won't mind—it sounds really cool.

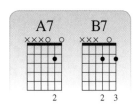

The change from Am to B7 isn't too tricky. Look at the diagrams to the right. You'll see that all you have to do to make the change is keep your second finger in place on the second fret of the second string, then remove the first finger and place the third finger on the second fret of the first string. Go back and forth between these chords in preparation for the song.

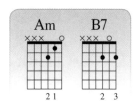

Finally, we introduce a new rhythm in the Am–C–A7–C sequence. The rhythm is a half note followed by two quarter notes. Be sure to count two beats for the half notes. Practice this rhythm using only the Em chord until you have it down. Notice that the rhythm changes back to quarter notes in the middle and then changes back again to the new rhythm at the end.

Now, have fun playing "Undercover."

UNDERCOVER

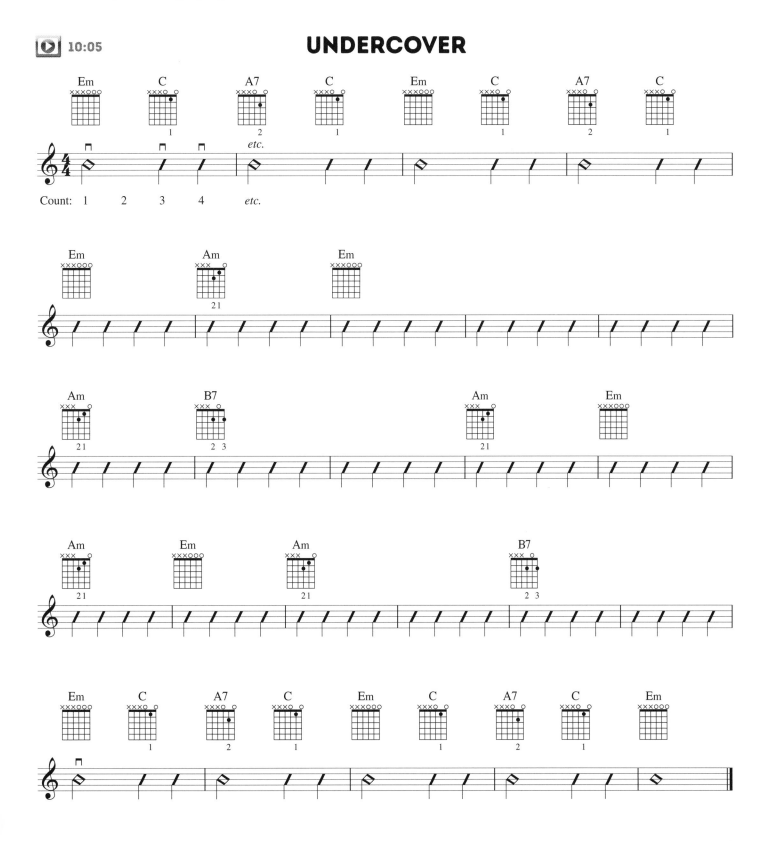

CHORDS ON THE TOP FOUR STRINGS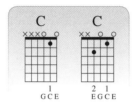

A NOTE ON VOICINGS

In this chapter, we will be strumming chords on the top four strings: strings 1–4. You'll notice that many of the chords are named the same as chords from the previous chapter. These are different *voicings* of the same basic chords. A voicing is a particular arrangement of the notes in a chord. For instance, a C chord is made up of the notes C, E, and G. These notes can be placed in any order and even doubled or tripled, and the chord will retain the same name and quality. As an example, the C chord in the previous chapter was made up of the notes G–C–E, from the third string to first. The C chord in this chapter consists of the notes E–G–C–E, from the fourth string to the first.

STRUMMING THE TOP FOUR STRINGS

Let's start by getting used to strumming the top four strings. The same mechanics used for strumming three strings applies here as well. Begin with your pick just above the fourth string and then sweep it downward through and just past the first string. Then bring the pick back to the starting position and strum again. The pick should be angled with the tip pointing upward to avoid any resistance against the strings. Without worrying about keeping proper time, repeat this process until you are comfortable with the strum.

WHOLE-, HALF- AND QUARTER-NOTE STRUMS

Once you have mastered the four-string strum, try it in time using the rhythm in Example 1. Remember, you are still strumming the open strings. As you will see, in addition to different voicings of chords, we will also be introducing different rhythms in this chapter. Example 1 includes a mix of whole-note, half-note, and quarter-note strums. Try it slowly at first, being sure to count aloud and steadily tap your foot. Like the previous chapter, you will be using all downstrokes for the following examples.

EXAMPLE 1 • 1:21

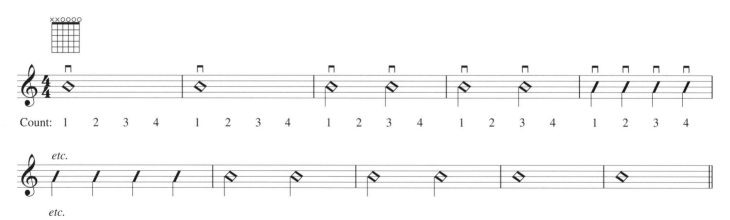

The next example, which is in the style of Nirvana's "Something in the Way," consists mostly of half- and quarter-note strums. Be sure to count, tap your foot, and keep a steady rhythm. Try playing the rhythm on the open strings before adding the chords. Your first two chords are Em and C. Notice that to change from the Em chord to C, all you need to do is keep your second finger in place and position the first finger on the first fret of the second string. Check out the chord diagrams below and then try Example 2.

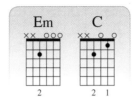

🔘 **EXAMPLE 2 (IN THE STYLE OF "SOMETHING IN THE WAY" BY NIRVANA)** • 2:48

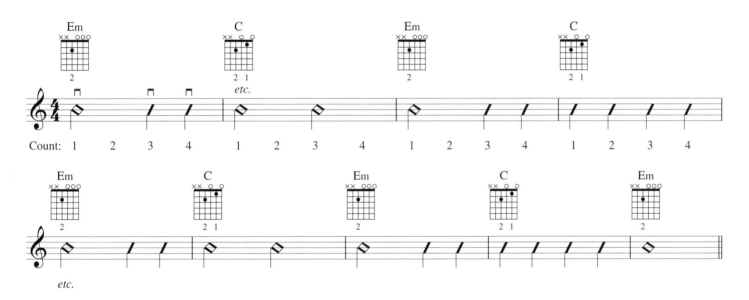

Now, we'll add one more chord, A7, to the progression. (A *chord progression* is a series of chords.) To switch from C to A7, keep your second finger in place on the second fret of the fourth string and place your third finger on the second fret of the second string. You can experiment by leaving the first finger in place on the first fret as you move to A7 or remove the finger entirely when switching to A7. Check out the A7 chord diagram to the right and then try Example 3. You'll notice it is a lot like the first four measures of "Undercover" on page 13.

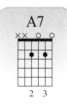

🔘 **EXAMPLE 3** • 3:54

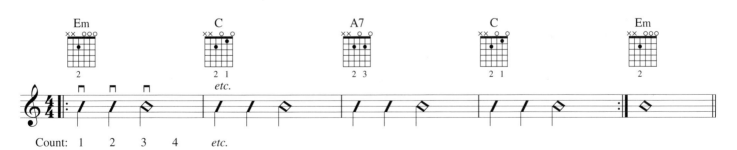

Below is an example with new voicings of G, Gmaj7, and G7. These are exactly like the fingerings in the previous chapter, except we are adding the open fourth string to each of them. Check out the chord diagrams and then try Example 4.

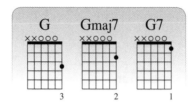

EXAMPLE 4 · 5:01

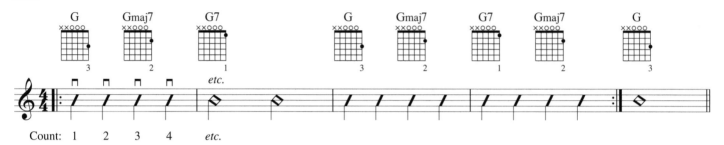

Here, we are adding C to the mix.

EXAMPLE 5 · 5:45

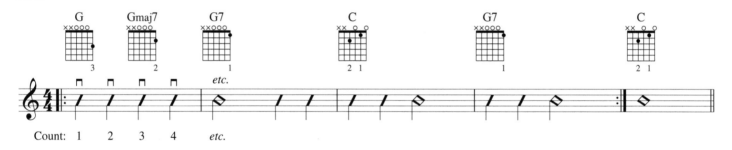

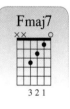

Next is "Camptown Races," a familiar tune by Stephen Foster. It consists of C, G7, and Fmaj7. Fmaj7 is a new chord, so spend a little time working on the fingering (see diagram to the right). Then, practice switching back and forth between C and Fmaj7, because they appear next to each other in the song. To change from C to Fmaj7, keep your first finger in place on the first fret of the second string and then simultaneously move your second finger to the second fret of the third string and your third finger to the third fret of the fourth string. Go back and forth between these two chords until you can do it without even thinking. The rhythm for this tune follows the rhythm for the melody, so you could easily sing along if desired. (Note: This song includes a *dotted half note*, which lasts for three beats. A *dot* increases the value of the note it follows by one half its original value: 2+1=3.)

CAMPTOWN RACES

Count: 1 2 3 4 *etc.*
Camp - town la - dies sing this song, doo - dah, doo - dah.

Measure numbers

Camp - town race - track five miles long. Oh, de doo - dah day.

Goin' to run all night. Goin' to run all day. I

bet my mon - ey on a bob - tail nag. Some - bod - y bet on the bay.

EIGHTH-NOTE STRUMS

Let's introduce eighth-note rhythms into our strumming. Remember that an eighth note lasts for one half of a beat, so it takes two of them to make one whole beat. Eighth notes are counted "1 & 2 & 3 & 4 &, 1 & 2 & 3 & 4 &," etc. In the next chapter, we will start using upstrokes as well as downstrokes, but for now, we will continue to use only downstrokes in order to get used to the different rhythms.

To begin, simply strum a steady eighth-note rhythm on the top four open strings. Do it slowly at first, being sure to count aloud and tap your foot. Your foot goes down on the *downbeats* (the numbers) and up on the *upbeats* (the &s).

EXAMPLE 6 · 8:29

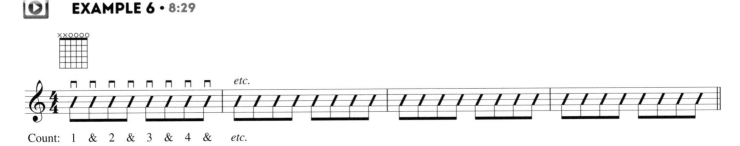

Count: 1 & 2 & 3 & 4 & *etc.*

Now, let's try an example using the C chord (or any chord of your choice). The point of Example 7 is to get you used to using the eighth-note strum in the context of other rhythms. This example also demonstrates the relationship between note values because it progresses from whole note to half notes, quarter notes, and eighth notes and then all the way back to a whole note. For the sake of this exercise, count all of the downbeats as well as upbeats in order to maintain awareness of the eighth-note rhythm throughout.

EXAMPLE 7 · 9:08

Example 8 introduces a four-string E chord (check out the diagram to the right). To switch from a C chord to an E chord, just keep your second finger in position on the second fret of the fourth string and move your first finger from the first fret of the second string to the first fret of the third string. Practice switching back and forth between those two chords and then try Example 8.

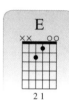

EXAMPLE 8 · 10:06

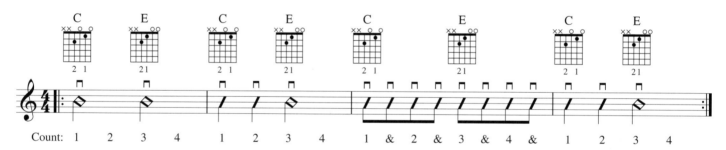

The next song has a driving rock feel because of the steady eighth-note strum and selection of chords. There are several things to be aware of when preparing to play it.

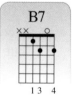

- There is a new chord, B7, on the third beat of measure 16. The fingering is a little tricky, so spend some time working on it. Check out the chord diagram to the right before moving on.

- Sometimes, you may choose to use a different fingering for chords you already know because of the context of the song. In other words, depending on the chords you are switching to, you may choose to use a different fingering to make the switches easier or more efficient.

- Two of the chord changes in "Eighth Note from the Sun" require moving only one finger—the switches from E to C and A7 to C. Similarly, the change from C to D7 requires you to keep the first finger in place on the first fret of the second string and move the other two fingers. Practice these first and then move on to the more challenging switches like G to A7 and G to D7.

- On beats 3 and 4 of measures 8 and 20, you are playing C and D7 for one beat each, so make sure you are particularly comfortable with that change. See the four-string D7 on the right.

- Also, make sure the eighth-note rhythm is completely steady. Use a metronome to ensure accuracy and just play the open strings again until you feel locked into the rhythm; then insert the chords.

EIGHTH NOTE FROM THE SUN

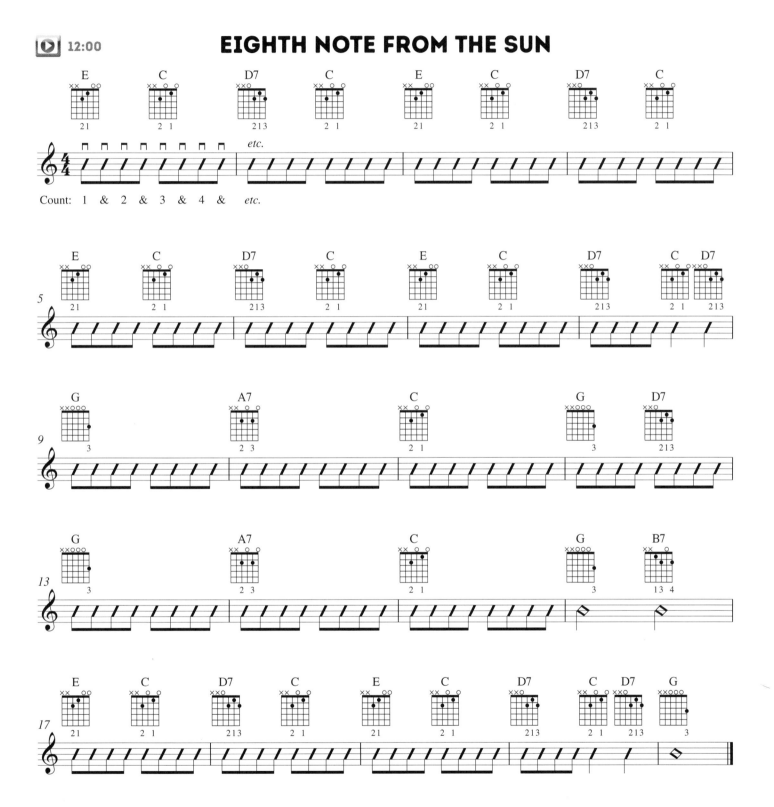

Let's practice the steady eighth-note strum some more. Example 9 has a driving rock feel as well, and the bass notes of the main three chords (the *bass note* is the lowest note of a chord) form a traditional rock bass line, the likes of which can be heard in Led Zeppelin's "Stairway to Heaven" among many other songs.

EXAMPLE 9 • 13:48

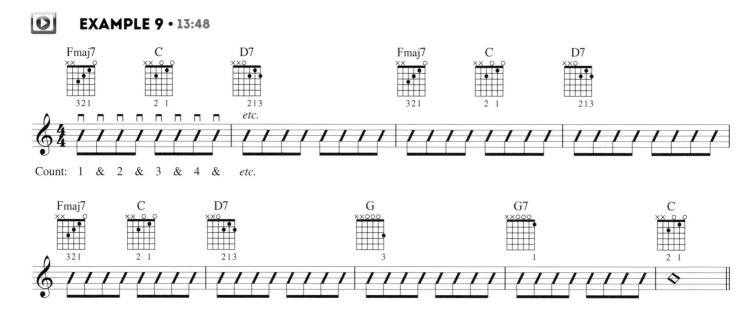

TRIPLET STRUMS

A *triplet* is a group of three notes in the time of two notes of the same value. An eighth-note triplet is made up of three eighth notes that take up the same value as two eighth notes—in other words, one beat. So, an eighth-note triplet divides a beat into three equal parts that are counted "1 & ah, 2 & ah, 3 & ah, 4 & ah," etc. Triplets are beamed together and have a "3" above or below the group. When tapping your foot, be sure to bring the foot down on the downbeats.

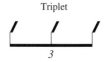

Following are a couple of examples and a song featuring the triplet strum.

Example 10 consists of a steady triplet strum on a C chord. Make sure you are strumming only the top four strings and use a metronome to develop good timing.

EXAMPLE 10 • 14:57

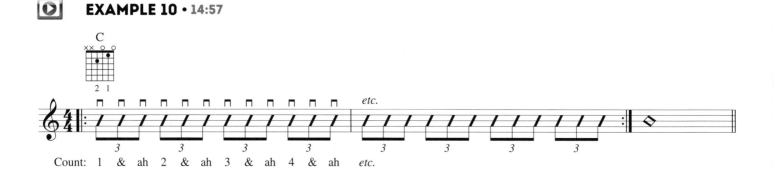

Next, for Example 11, we'll play the same triplet rhythm and add a four-string Am chord (see right). The switch between C and Am is easy: just keep the first and second fingers in place and add the third finger to the second fret of the third string. Practice switching between the two chords and then try it using the triplet rhythm as demonstrated in the example below.

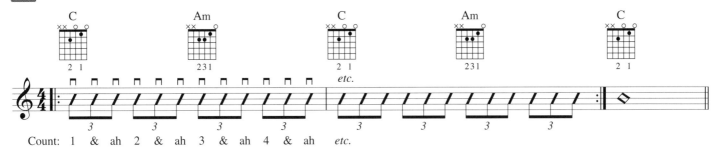

The following song, which features our triplet strum, begins with the C to Am chord change from Example 11 and then moves into some other changes that should be no problem with a little practice. This chord progression has been used in many tunes throughout the years, especially the 1950s. "Fifties Unchained" is in the style of "Unchained Melody," made famous by the Righteous Brothers. Keep the rhythm steady and enjoy playing this classic-sounding tune.

FIFTIES UNCHAINED

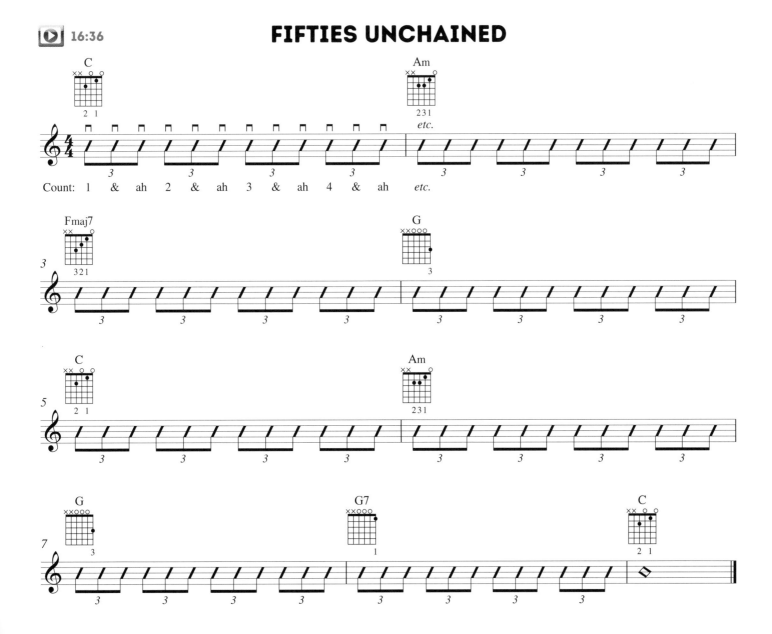

Following is a 12-bar blues progression in the *key* of D. A key is a kind of tonal "home base." A song often begins and ends on the chord named after the key. For instance, "Four-String Blues in D" starts and ends with a D chord (specifically, D7). The triplet rhythm is an integral part of the blues, so it is featured here. Try *accenting*, or emphasizing, the second and fourth downbeats of each measure by playing the first eighth notes of those groups just a little louder than the others. Remember to use nice, even strums. Tap your foot on the downbeats and count as follows: "1 & ah **2** & ah 3 & ah **4** & ah."

> = Accent

FOUR-STRING BLUES IN D

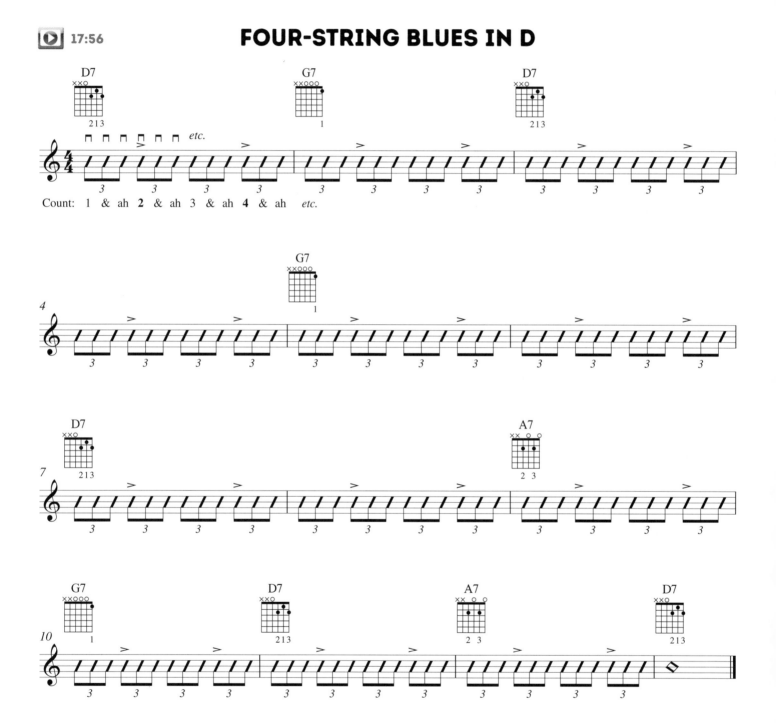

STRUMS WITH TIES

A *tie* is a curved line that connects two notes of the same pitch (or, in this case, two chords of the same pitch). When two notes are tied, their value is the first note plus the value of the second. So, if a quarter note is tied to a quarter note, the combined value is two beats—or the same as a half note. The first note is sounded and continues to ring for the duration of the second note; there is no pick attack on the second note. An eighth note tied to an eighth note rings out for the combined value of one beat. Let's try an example.

In Example 12, the eighth note on the "&" of beat 2 is tied to the eighth note on the downbeat of beat 3. So, in this case, you would keep the strings ringing after strumming the "&" of beat 2, but you wouldn't strum again until the "&" of beat 3. Start by playing a steady eighth-note strum until comfortable. Then, while maintaining an even rhythm, simply skip the strum on the downbeat of beat 3. Once again, keep your counting steady and strum every eighth note except the downbeat of beat 3. OK, now give it a shot.

▶ EXAMPLE 12 • 19:41

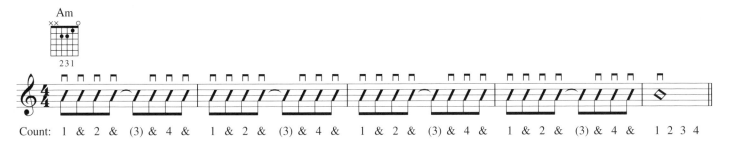

▶ EXAMPLE 13 (IN THE STYLE OF "STAIRWAY TO HEAVEN" BY LED ZEPPELIN) • 20:23

Our next example is in the style of the last part of Led Zeppelin's epic song "Stairway to Heaven." First, strum the rhythm using only the Am chord so you get the feel of it before you start working on the chord changes. Only the second and fourth measures have ties, where the "&" of beat 2 is tied to the downbeat of beat 3. Once the rhythm is comfortable, make sure you have your switching down. The trickiest changes appear in the same measures as the ties—on beat 4 of measures 2 and 4, you switch to the G chord for one beat and then to Am on the first downbeat of the next measure. Enjoy this cool progression.

▶ EXAMPLE 13 (IN THE STYLE OF "STAIRWAY TO HEAVEN" BY LED ZEPPELIN) • 20:23

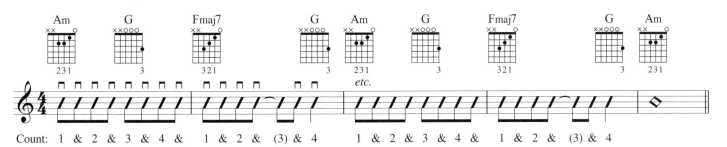

Check out the chord diagram to the right, which shows how to play a new chord, Dm. You can experiment by replacing the third finger with the pinky—both are standard fingerings, and you should choose whichever is most comfortable for you in any given situation. The chord changes are fairly easy in Example 14—especially the change from Dm to G7, where you just remove your second and third fingers to play the G7 chord. Make sure you have all the changes in place and then look at the rhythm. In each measure, the tie occurs from the "&" of beat 3 to the downbeat of beat 4. So, keep the chord ringing, but skip the strum on the downbeat of beat 4. Practice the rhythm using only a single chord and then play the example as written. (Note: Typically, this particular tied eighth-note rhythm would be written in notation as a single quarter note on the "&" of beat 3, instead of two tied eighths.)

EXAMPLE 14 · 21:35

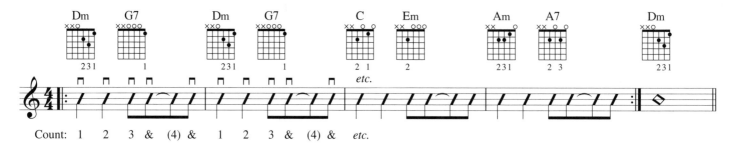

Our final song of the chapter is in the style of David Bowie's "Space Oddity." When preparing to play it, keep the following considerations in mind.

- There is one new chord to learn, A, but there are two fingerings used to make certain changes easier. One fingering uses the second, third, and fourth fingers, and the other uses the first, second, and third fingers. Both are pictured below.

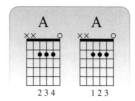

You'll notice that measure 21 uses the 2-3-4 fingering. This option is used because the second finger is already in place for the Em chord right before it, so all you need to do is place the third and fourth fingers. Then, the following chord is C. For this, you just keep the second finger in place and simultaneously remove the third finger and place the first finger on the first fret of the second string. In measures 23 and 24, it makes more sense to use the 1-2-3 fingering, because you can simply place all three fingers at once. The A chord can be tricky, but make sure you angle your wrist slightly to accommodate all three fingers at the same fret. Also, be sure all the notes are ringing out clearly—if they are not, move the offending finger (or fingers) closer to the second fret if possible.

- The predominant rhythm features a tie from the "&" of beat 2 to the downbeat of beat 3. This is a very common rock and pop rhythm.

- Measures 23–24 feature some quick changes. First, you play C and Fmaj7 for a beat each. Next, you play G for a half beat then switch to A for an eighth note and a quarter note.

OCEAN ANOMALY

Count: 1 2 & (3) & 4 & *etc.*

Congratulations! You have aced playing chords on the top four strings. In the next chapter, we move on to five-string chords.

In this chapter, we'll cover five-string voicings for chords discussed in the previous chapter, and these will be played along with some four-string voicings as well. Plus, you will start alternating strumming directions so that you can begin applying this technique to a variety of great-sounding strumming patterns.

STRUMMING THE TOP FIVE STRINGS

Let's get used to strumming strings 1–5. Begin with your pick just above the fifth string and then sweep it downward through and just past the first string. Then bring the pick back to the starting position and strum again. Remember, the pick should be angled with the tip pointing upward so that it glides smoothly across the strings. Once you feel comfortable with the basic mechanics, try strumming the following rhythm.

▶ EXAMPLE 1 · 0:36

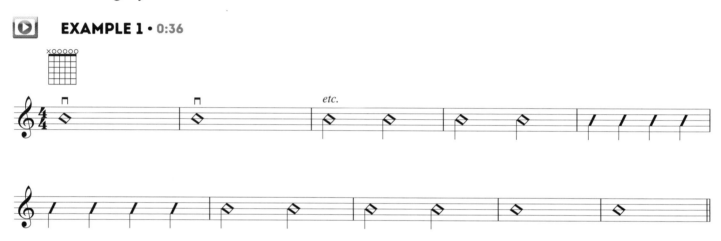

NEW VOICINGS AND STRUM PATTERN 1

Nearly everything in this book is played in *open position*, and, generally, what that means is that the chords include open strings and are located within the first four frets of the guitar. All the chords in this chapter are considered standard open-position voicings. We have worked our way up from three strings to four strings and now to five strings in order to get you playing the chords quicker. We will progress to standard six-string chords in the next chapter, and, by that time, you'll be thoroughly prepared for those bigger voicings.

Following, we'll look at new voicings for the chords C, A, Am, and A7. In addition, we will introduce a new chord, C7. To familiarize ourselves with the new chord forms, we'll use a straight quarter-note strum, which, from this point forward, we'll refer to as **Strum Pattern 1**.

In Example 2, we have the five-string voicings for Am and C. Both of these are the most common open-position fingerings for these chords. The Am chord should look familiar because it uses the same fingers and locations as the four-chord voicing in the previous chapter. The only difference here is that you include the open fifth (A) string. The C chord starts with the four-string fingering and adds the third finger to the third fret of the fifth string. Check out the diagrams to the right and, not following any particular rhythm, practice switching back and forth between the two chords. To do this, just move your third finger from the second fret of the third string (for Am) to the third fret of the fifth string (for C)—back and forth.

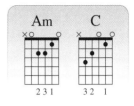

Now try Example 2, which starts by having you switch chords every measure and then increases the *harmonic rhythm* (the frequency at which chords change) until you are switching on every quarter note; this is a good workout to increase dexterity.

EXAMPLE 2 · 2:12

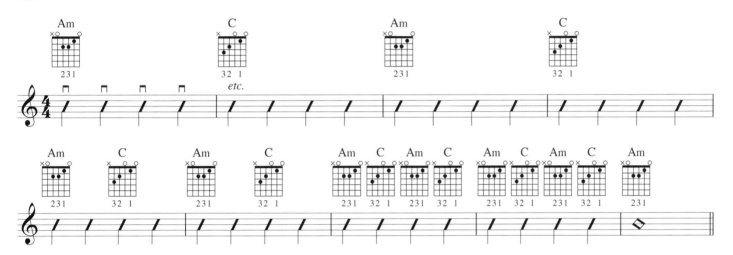

Next is an example featuring the C and C7 chords. Check out the C7 diagram to the right and then practice switching back and forth between the two chords. This change is even easier than the previous one, because all you need to do is add the pinky to the third fret of the third string to get a C7 chord. Practice switching between the two and then try Example 3, which features the same harmonic rhythm as Example 2.

EXAMPLE 3 · 3:15

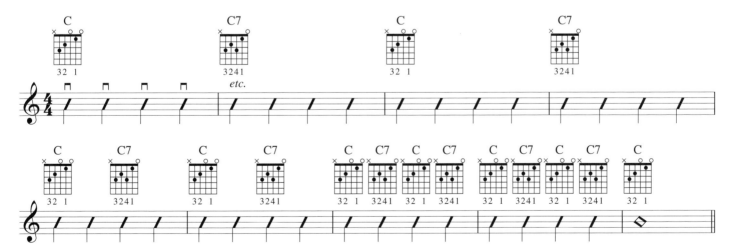

Example 4 features two more voicings that are very similar to their four-string counterparts: A and A7. Both of these chords have the exact same fingering as the four-string versions except they include the open fifth (A) string. These are the standard open-string voicings for these chords because they have the *root note* as the lowest note in the chord. (The root is the note upon which the chord is built and from which it gets its name.) To change from A to A7, you could simply remove your second finger, but let's get used to the more common fingering: remove your first finger and place the second finger on the second fret of the fourth string. Practice this change and then try Example 4, which consists of the same harmonic rhythm as the previous two examples.

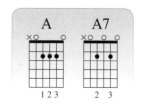

EXAMPLE 4 • 4:37

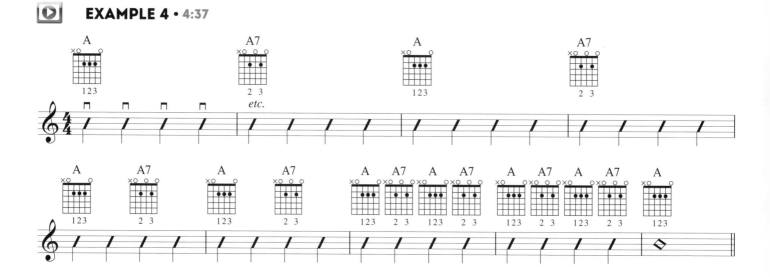

Following is an example that combines the new fingerings introduced in this chapter. Most of the chord changes are fairly simple, but A to Am requires all of the fingers to change positions. Here is a method you can use to practice changes like this:

1. Form the A chord with the fretting-hand fingers.

2. Lift the fingers directly up from the fretboard, still in the form of an A chord, but now hovering above the frets.

3. In mid-air, form the Am chord with your fingers and then bring them down, together, to the appropriate strings and frets.

4. Lift the fingers off the fretboard, still in the form of an Am chord.

5. In mid-air, form the A chord and then bring your fingers down to their proper positions on the fretboard.

6. Do this over and over until you have mastered this switch.

Soon, you will be able to start forming the new chord as soon as you lift the fingers from the frets, but be patient—this will take time.

The change from A to C can also be practiced using the method above.

However, an easier option at this point is to use the 2-3-4 fingering for the A chord. Then you can keep your second and third fingers down for the change to Am. Now, try the example on the next page.

 **EXAMPLE 5 • 6:17**

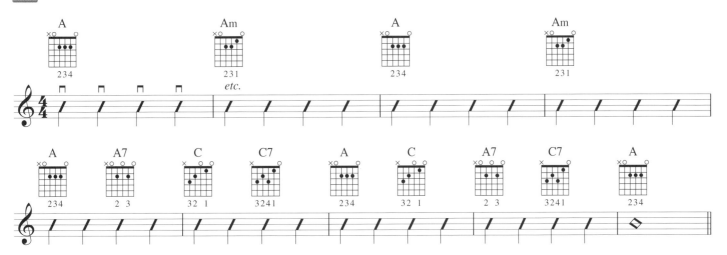

THE ALTERNATING STRUM AND STRUM PATTERN 2

Up until this point, you have only been strumming downward. Now, we'll introduce the *alternating strum,* where you will strum down-up-down-up (⊓ ∨ ⊓ ∨), etc.

HOW TO DO IT

In the same way you angle the pick upward on the downward strums in order to facilitate a smooth sweeping motion across the strings, angle the point of the pick downward when executing upstrums. If the tip of the pick is pointing directly at the strings, it will get caught in them, and the smooth motion will be impossible. Check out the photos below for correct and incorrect pick angles.

Correct pick angle for downstrum

Correct pick angle for upstrum

Incorrect pick angle for strumming

Practice the alternating strum slowly and evenly with the open strings. You'll notice that your hand makes a slight figure-8 motion to accommodate the changing angle of the pick. Don't worry about starting precisely at the fifth string on the downstrum or ending precisely at the fifth string on the upstrum. This will sound stiff and unpleasant. In fact, on the upstrum, it is OK to even just strum the top few strings. This process should sound and feel natural.

STRUM PATTERN 2

Now, try the example below. In this book, a consistent alternating eighth-note strum will be referred to as **Strum Pattern 2**.

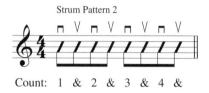

EXAMPLE 6 • 8:00

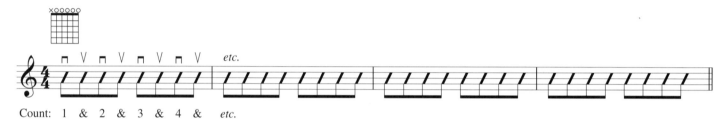

OK, now let's try the pattern with some actual chords. Remember that, on the upstrum, it's only necessary to hit the top few strings. Don't try to hit precisely five strings on every strum. Keep the motion smooth and loose. The next example is in the style of Bob Marley's "Three Little Birds." To switch from A and D, slide your third finger up from the second fret of the second string to the third fret and then place the other fingers accordingly. Check out the new chord D on the right.

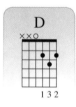

EXAMPLE 7 (IN THE STYLE OF BOB MARLEY'S "THREE LITTLE BIRDS") • 8:32

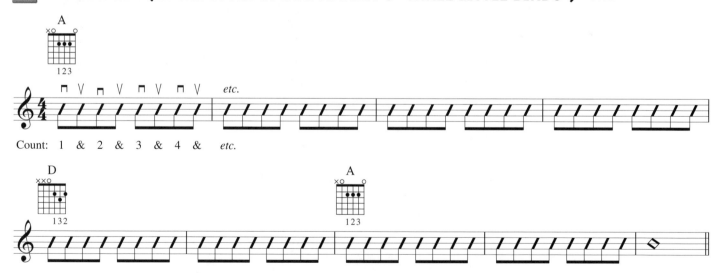

Example 8 features a chord progression used in many songs, including the end section of Lynyrd Skynyrd's "Freebird." Give it a try. Remember to keep the strum light and steady.

EXAMPLE 8 • 9:13

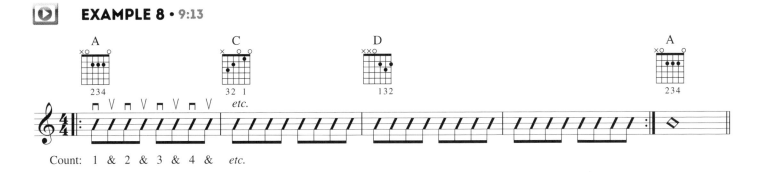

Our next tune is in the style of Bob Dylan's "Hurricane," and it should be played at a fairly quick pace. Following are some pointers and ideas to keep in mind while practicing this one.

1. At this point, don't struggle for precision when it comes to hitting exactly five strings. On the upstrum, in particular, just lightly strum the top few.

2. We are using **Strum Pattern 2** for the whole song, except for beats 3 and 4 of measure 16, where you are changing chords on each beat.

3. In measures 1–12, keep your first finger in place on the first fret of the second string. Just change the other fingers accordingly for the various chords.

4. **Very important:** When strumming eighth notes, it may sound forced to reposition your fingers for a new chord precisely at the time of the switch. For example, if you were to keep the fingers in place for Am through every eighth note in the first measure and then try to switch them right before the first eighth note of the second measure, it would sound kind of stiff—not to mention a challenge to execute. The remedy for this is to lift the fingers that need to be changed on the last eighth note of a measure and start to reposition them so that they are easily in place on the first eighth note of the next measure. So, the change actually starts happening on the last eighth note, as indicated in Example 9 below. Remember, it is OK to hear the open strings on those last upbeats as you change chords. It actually creates a smooth, natural feel to the transitions.

EXAMPLE 9 • 10:27

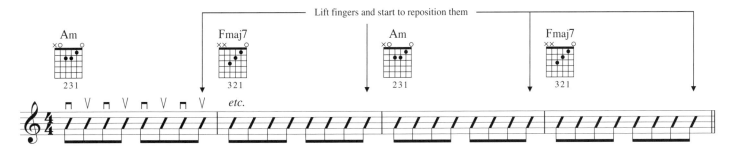

Keep the above considerations in mind and begin working on "Cyclone."

CYCLONE

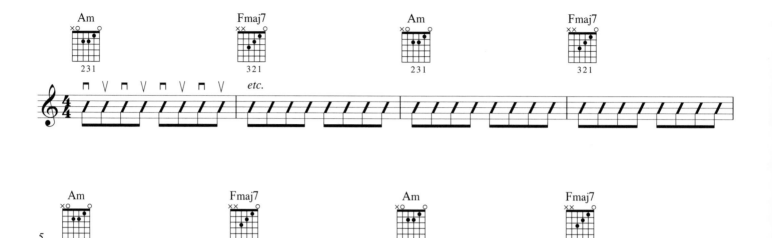

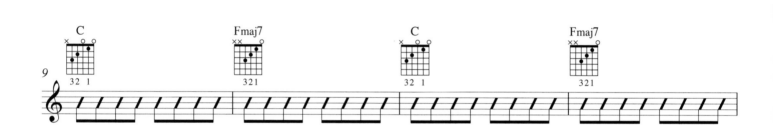

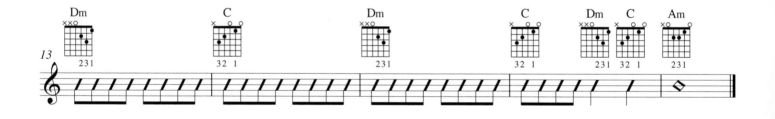

The last song of the chapter is in the style of "(I'm Not Your) Steppin' Stone" made famous by the Monkees. You already worked on the changes from A to C to D in Example 8, so that shouldn't be a problem. As mentioned for "Cyclone," set up your chord changes on the eighth note immediately preceding where the change is actually supposed to occur. This will become challenging in measures 9–14 when you begin changing every two beats, but especially on beats 3 and 4 of measure 16, where you switch on each beat. Be sure to practice making these changes as smooth and flowing as possible.

SKIPPING ROCKS

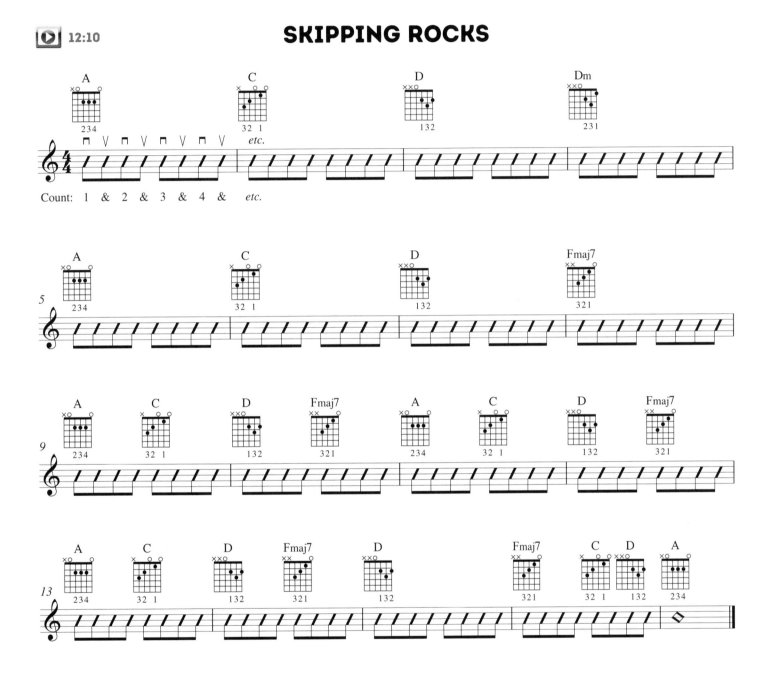

CHORDS ON ALL SIX STRINGS

Chapter 4 introduces six-string chords and several new strum patterns and techniques.

STRUMMING ALL SIX STRINGS

The technique for strumming six strings is quite easy, especially if you've already made it this far. Start with your pick just above the sixth string and sweep downward through the first string. Keep the tip of the pick angled upward for the downstroke and then execute the slight figure-8 with the wrist to angle the tip of the pick downward for the upstroke. For the moment, strum all six strings on the upstrokes as well, but be sure to maintain a light, smooth, and steady motion and strum. Try the following example to get used to the feel.

EXAMPLE 1 · 0:21

STRUM PATTERN 3 AND NEW SIX-STRING VOICINGS

Strum Pattern 3 features alternate strumming on beats 2 and 4. It is important to maintain the down-up motion of your strumming hand throughout, even when you are not striking the strings on a particular upbeat—the steady wrist and forearm movement is: down-up-down-up, etc.

In the first measure of Example 2, the upbeats that are *not* to be strummed are indicated by an "&" in parentheses and a "V" in parentheses. At first, count all the downbeats and upbeats; then count as indicated in measure 2. This example uses only open strings so you can concentrate on the strumming hand.

EXAMPLE 2 · 1:10

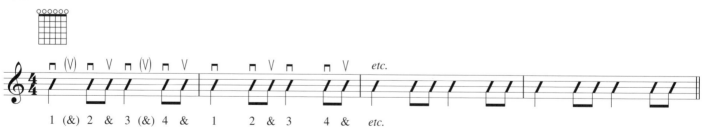

Let's introduce some chords into the new strum pattern. Example 3 features six-string voicings for Em and G. The Em fingering is straightforward, but the G chord is a bit more challenging. Try the Em fingering below and then move on to G. We'll consider the first fingering for G our standard fingering, because it allows for smooth transitions to many other chords (Em, for example). Fingering 1 employs a stretch between the third and fourth fingers, which, for some players may seem a bit awkward or difficult. Practice this fingering, because it makes many chord changes more efficient than when using the second fingering. Fingering 2 is possibly easier to play on its own, but in the context of various chord changes, it is often not the best choice. Try both fingerings and choose the option that works best for you.

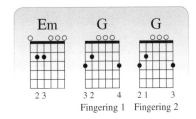

In Example 3, you are switching between Em and G. (We'll use the first fingering for G, but you can try the second.) To change from Em to G, keep your second finger in place on the second fret of the fifth string, and then move your third finger to the third fret of the sixth string and place your pinky on the third fret of the first string. Go back and forth between the two chords a few times and then try the change using **Strum Pattern 3**, as written below. At first, you are switching chords at every new measure; then you change every two beats and conclude by returning to one change per measure.

EXAMPLE 3 · 2:19

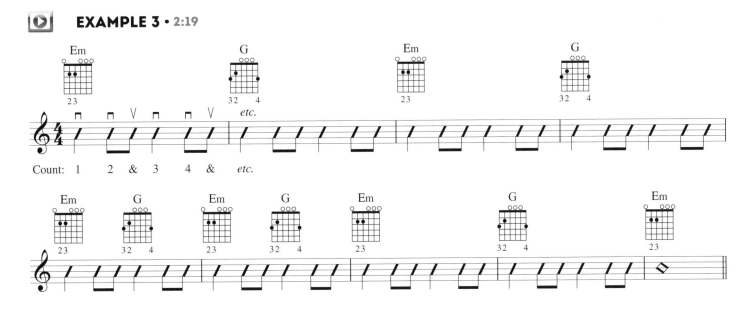

Example 4 features three new voicings: G7, E, and E7 (see diagrams below). The switch between G and G7 is simple—just leave your second and third fingers in place, remove the pinky, and place the first finger on the first fret of the first string. To change between G7 and E, leave your second finger in place and then move the other fingers accordingly. The switch between E and E7 is easy as well—simply remove the third finger. Finally, to go from E7 to G, keep your second finger in place on the second fret of the fifth string and then move the other fingers to the appropriate locations. Like the previous example, we'll start by changing chords once per measure and then increase the harmonic rhythm as we go. Remember to count out loud and tap your foot on the downbeats until you are thoroughly accustomed to **Strum Pattern 3**. Also, strum lightly and evenly. Check out the new chords on the right and then try Example 4.

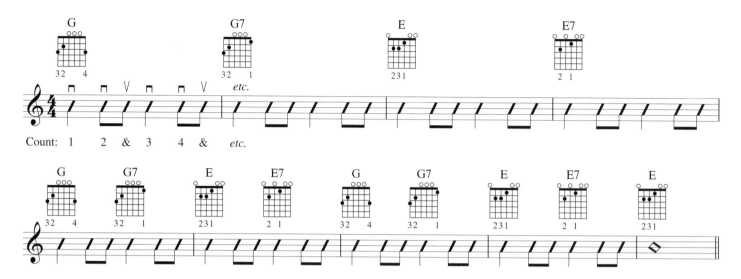

FOUR- AND FIVE-STRING VOICINGS AND FRET-HAND MUTING

We have looked at several different voicings for common chords. Some of them were introduced, like the three-string versions, to get you strumming quickly. Others are considered standard open-position fingerings. At the end of this chapter, for your reference, we will compile the forms we have looked at so far that are considered standard. The chords we are discussing below refer to the standard, or most common, forms.

Strumming six-string chords is easy, because you are sounding *all* the strings—you don't have to skip any or start at the fourth or fifth string. However, four- and five-string voicings present the following considerations.

FOUR-STRING VOICINGS

The four-string chords we have looked at that are considered standard are D, Dm, D7, and Fmaj7. It is essential when playing these chords to avoid the sixth string, E, because that note clashes with the other notes. However, it is acceptable, if you so choose, to include the fifth string—because the A note does not clash with the other chord tones and is, in fact, already being played elsewhere in the voicing. This will produce a slightly different sound because the root note is no longer in the bass, but often this sound is acceptable and sometimes even preferable. So, here are the diagrams rewritten to show this new option. (The open fifth string is indicated with parentheses.)

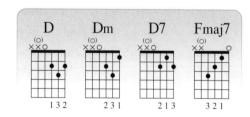

FIVE-STRING VOICINGS

The standard five-string chords we have looked at so far are A, Am, A7, C, and C7. It is acceptable (and sometimes preferable) to include the sixth string when strumming these chords, because the E note is a part of all of them. However, because the chord's root note is no longer in the bass, these chords will have a different sound. Experiment on your own to hear the difference.

Below are chord diagrams rewritten to show this option.

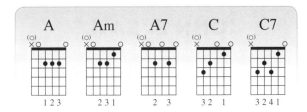

FRET-HAND MUTING

It's not easy to strum freely when we are trying to avoid the sixth string with our pick, but *fret-hand muting* provides a solution. Wrap the fretting-hand thumb around the neck and lightly touch the sixth string so that it deadens, or *mutes,* the string. This allows us to strum all the strings freely without worrying about skipping the sixth. Check out the photos below, which demonstrate the proper thumb position for muting the sixth string.

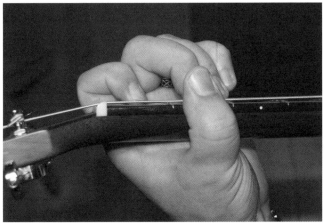

Correct thumb position for muting (top view)   *Correct thumb position for muting (front view)*

Keep the sixth string muted throughout the following exercise.

EXAMPLE 5 • 4:50

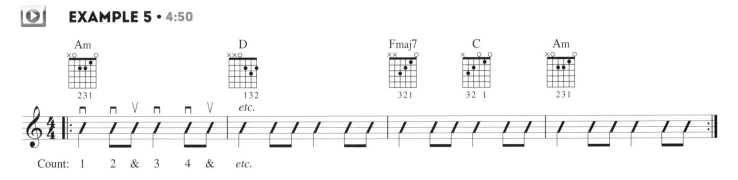

To strum as freely as possible, it is usually advisable to apply this muting technique on four- and five-strings voicings. Keep this in mind when working on the rest of this book.

The last example of this section is the classic folk song "John B. Sails." This tune has been recorded by many artists throughout the years, including the famous version by the Beach Boys under the title "Sloop John B."

"John B. Sails" features **Strum Pattern 3** and six-string chords (G and G7). There is also a four-string voicing (D) and two five-string fingerings (C and Am). Use the fretting-hand muting technique for the four- and five-string chords.

JOHN B. SAILS

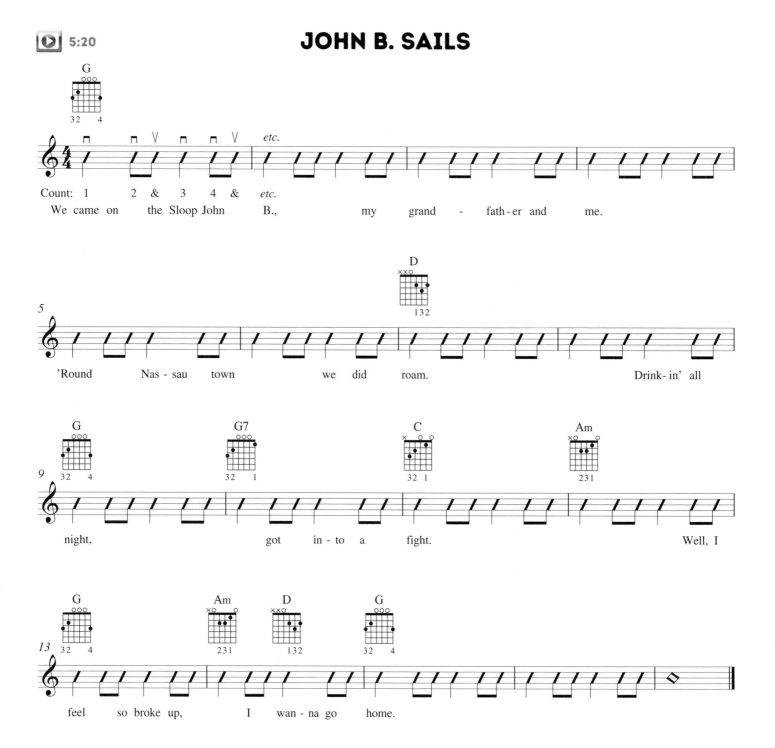

TONAL CONSIDERATIONS

There are many factors for producing different tonal qualities in your playing. Following are some of the most important.

STRINGS

- Lighter-gauge strings are easier to press against the frets but produce a thinner, jangly kind of sound.

- Heavier-gauge strings, though a bit harder to press against the frets, produce a richer, "fatter" tone.

FINGERS OR PICKS

- Using fingers to strum produces a warm, mellow, quieter tone.

- When using a pick, a sharper, almost percussive effect is created, because you can hear each attack of the pick on the strings, and the point of contact is more precise than with your thumb or fingers. The lighter the pick, the more percussive the sound. Heavier picks do not produce as much of a percussive effect, but you can strike the strings with more force.

STRUMMING LOCATION

- **Over the sound hole:** This is the standard location or "home base" for your strumming. It represents a tonal middle ground that is not too jangly and not particularly mellow. It is a great location from which to add variety to your tone when appropriate. (See Photo 1 below.)

- **Near the bridge:** The closer to the bridge you strum, the more trebly, tinny, or higher-end the tone. The classical term for this location is *sul ponticello*. (See Photo 2 below.)

- **Over the fretboard:** The closer to the fretboard you strum, even directly above the fretboard just past the sound hole, the mellower the tone. The classical term for this location is *sul tasto*. (See Photo 3 below.)

Try any example in this book, preferably an easy quarter-note strum, and experiment with these different strumming locations. You will be amazed at the breadth of tonal variety available to you just by striking the strings in different places. Below are photos showing each of the three strumming locations.

Photo 1: Over the sound hole

Photo 2: Near the bridge

Photo 3: Over the fretboard

STRUM PATTERN 4

Strum Pattern 4 features alternate strumming on beats 2, 3, and 4. As when learning **Strum Pattern 3**, maintain the down-up motion of your strumming hand throughout, even when you are not striking the strings on the "&" of beat 1 (indicated in the first measure by an "&" and "∨" in parentheses). At first, count all the downbeats and upbeats; then count as indicated in measure 2. This example uses only open strings so you can concentrate on the strum.

EXAMPLE 6 • 7:24

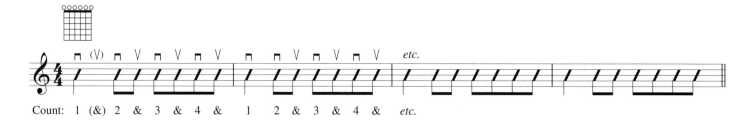

Example 7 features two new voicings (see diagrams to the right). The first is Am7 in measure 4, and the other is an alternate fingering for E7 in measure 6. For the new E7 fingering, maintain the E chord and place the pinky on the third fret of the second string. In measures 1–4, the changes from E to E7 and Am to Am7 are very similar—in each case, simply remove the third finger from the first chord to sound the second. Also, don't forget to use fret-hand muting on the four- and five-string voicings—you especially need to mute the sixth string on the final D chord.

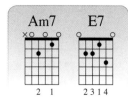

EXAMPLE 7 • 8:21

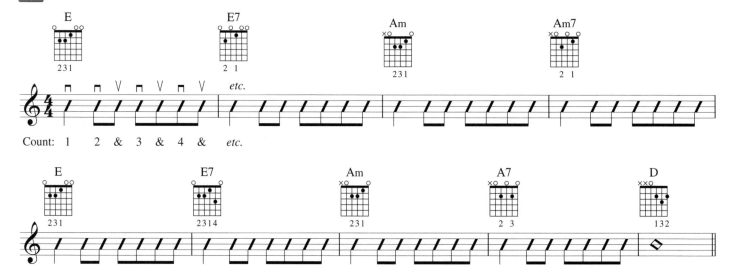

Next is a popular song that is a lot of fun to play and sing. "Drunken Sailor" is a sea shanty from the 1820s that was sung aboard British ships to accompany certain tasks. Play this at a brisk tempo—about 150 beats per minute.

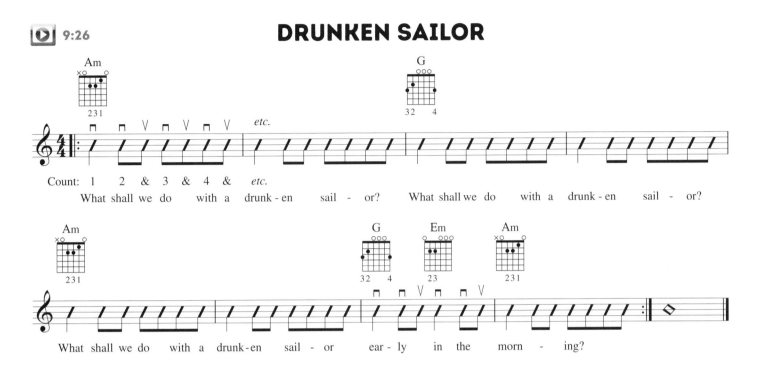

DRUNKEN SAILOR

"Movin' Down the Road" should also be played at a brisk tempo of about 156 beats per minute. Keep the strum steady and don't be afraid to dig into this one a bit. Following are some other considerations to keep in mind.

1. Notice the brackets above measures 8 and 9. The "1" signifies the *first ending*, and the "2" signifies the *second ending*. When you get to the repeat sign in measure 8, go back to the beginning and repeat. The second time through, skip over measure 8 to the second ending and play to the end.

2. We have a new voicing for B7 (see diagram below). It is important to mute the sixth string when playing this chord. You can do this using the fret-hand thumb—as we have discussed—or, you can touch the string with the fret-hand second finger that is fretting the second fret of the fifth string. Check out the photo demonstrating this new muting technique.

Muting with the second finger

3. Use **Strum Pattern 4** except for measures 9 and 17 (which call for **Strum Pattern 3**) and measure 25 (which consists of two half notes).

10:53

MOVIN' DOWN THE ROAD

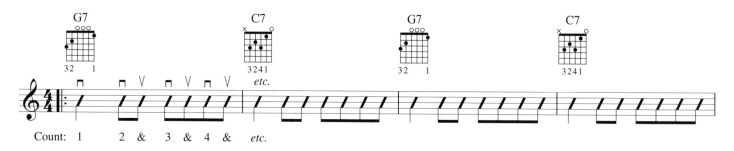

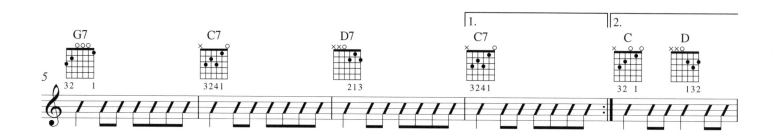

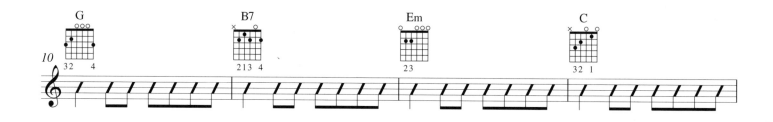

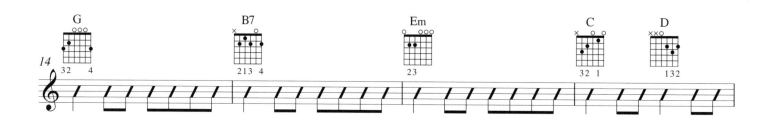

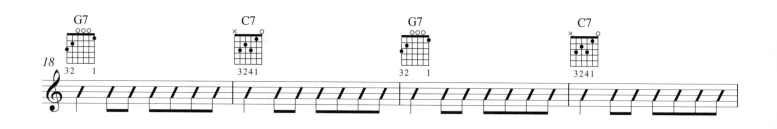

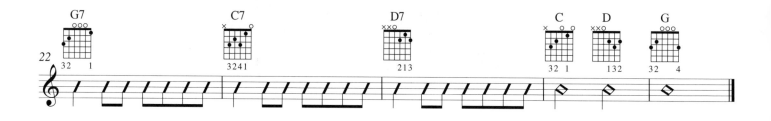

STRUM PATTERN 5

We first encountered the rhythm for **Strum Pattern 5** in "Ocean Anomaly" (page 25). In that song, we used downstrokes only, but now we'll incorporate alternate strumming. The tricky part about this rhythm is that the eighth note on the "&" of beat 2 is tied to the eighth note on the downbeat of beat 3. So, you do not strum on the downbeat, but on the "&" of beat 3. Keep the strumming arm in constant down-up motion, yet strum only in the indicated places. In measure 1, the upstrokes and downstrokes to be skipped are in parentheses. The corresponding locations in the counting numbers are also in parentheses. We'll start with open strings to get used to the strum. Be sure to count aloud and tap your foot on the downbeats.

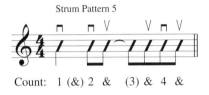

 **EXAMPLE 8 • 12:24**

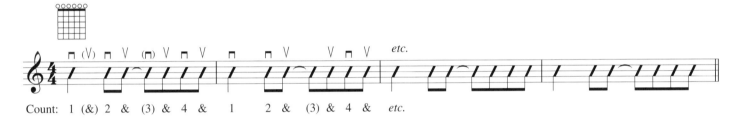

Example 9 is in the style of George Harrison's "My Sweet Lord." Make sure you are comfortable with the strum pattern so that you can make smooth chord changes without breaking from the rhythm.

 **EXAMPLE 9 (IN THE STYLE OF "MY SWEET LORD" BY GEORGE HARRISON) • 12:47**

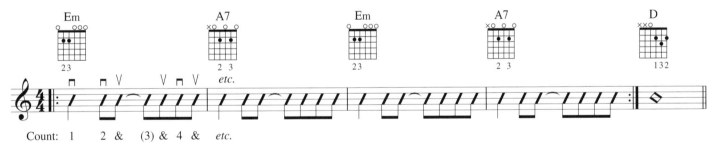

The last example in this chapter is a song in the style of "Good Riddance (Time of Your Life)" by Green Day. It features a new fingering for G and two new chords: Cadd9 and Dsus2. Check out the diagrams below.

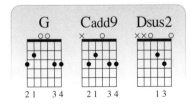

This new fingering for G has a rich, full sound and was used a lot by Led Zeppelin guitarist Jimmy Page, among many others. Also, it works nicely with the Cadd9 chord that follows it in this song, because you leave the third and fourth fingers in place and maintain the shape formed by the first and second fingers while moving them from the fifth and sixth strings to the fourth and fifth strings. Dsus2 is like a D chord but without the second finger.

This song has you switching from D to Dsus2 on the "&" of beat 2 and then back to D on the "&" of beat 3. This change is easy (as pointed out above) because all you need to do is remove the second finger for Dsus2 and then place it back in position for D. However, the tricky part is that the changes occur on the upbeats. When emphasis is shifted from the downbeats to the upbeats, it is referred to as *syncopation*. **Strum Pattern 5** is a perfect example of a syncopated rhythm, and switching chords on the upbeat accentuates the syncopated feel. This change first occurs in measure 4—practice it over and over until you get it right.

Remember to mute the sixth string on those four- and five-string voicings!

14:03

GOOD TIMES, GOOD TIMES

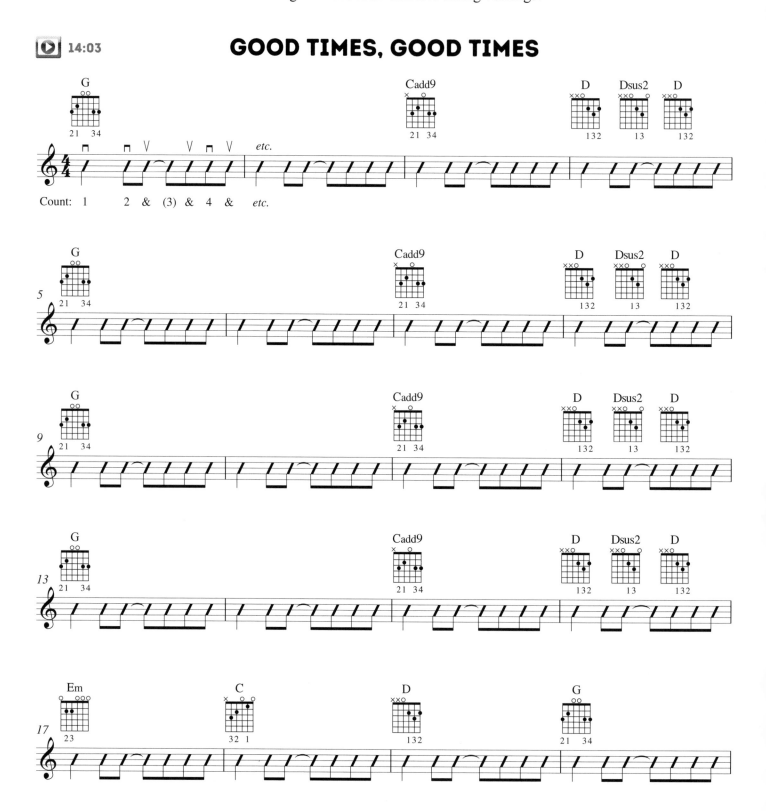

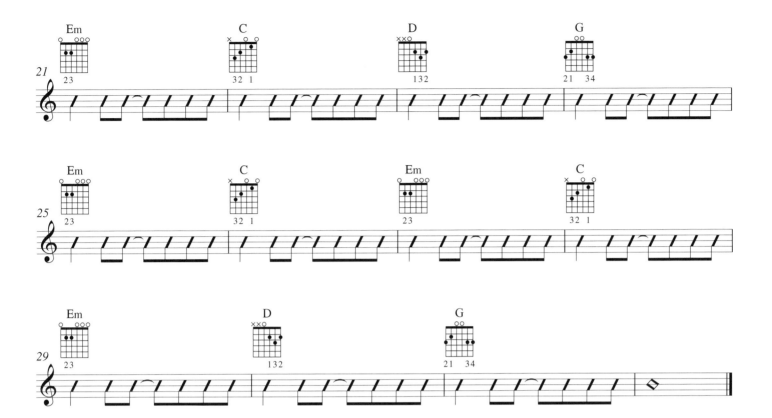

MOST COMMON VOICINGS

We have looked at a lot of different voicings so far, from three-string versions to six-string. Some of the voicings are more widely used than others. For reference and review before moving on, following are some of the most common, or standard, fingerings.

FOUR-STRING VOICINGS

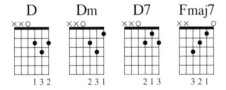

FIVE-STRING VOICINGS

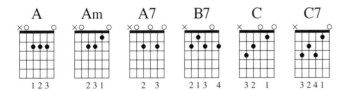

SIX-STRING VOICINGS

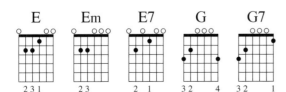

CHAPTER 5
SWING RHYTHM ▶

The *swing rhythm* is essential to blues, jazz, folk, pop, and other types of music. What determines the feel of this rhythm is how the eighth notes are played. The feel we have been using so far can be referred to as *straight eighths*, but the eighth notes played with a swing rhythm are *swung eighths*, or *swing eighths*. Swing eighths have a triplet feel—in fact, they are played like a triplet with the first two notes tied together. However, they are written as regular eighth notes, and the swing rhythm is indicated with a descriptor at the beginning of the music, such as "Swing 8ths" or the symbol below:

To get used to this rhythm, start by playing triplets, strumming down-down-up, down-down-up. After playing this for a couple of measures, skip the second downstrum, but let the first strum ring for the duration of the first two notes in each triplet. Now, you will be strumming down-up, down-up, and the eighth notes will have a skipping feel: long-short, long-short, etc. Give Example 1 a try.

▶ **EXAMPLE 1 • 1:14**

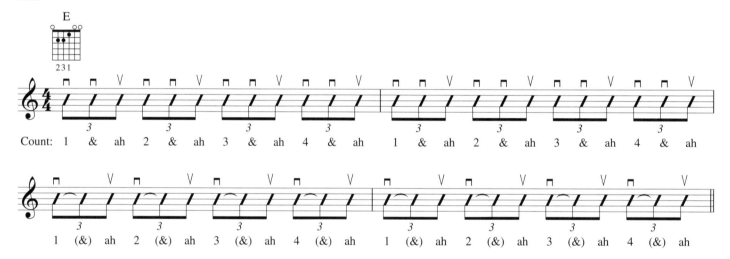

SWING EIGHTHS APPLIED TO THE STRUM PATTERNS

The swing rhythm can be applied to any strum pattern that includes eighth notes. Following are examples of **Strum Patterns 2–5** played using swing eighths.

STRUM PATTERN 2

Example 2 features **Strum Pattern 2** with a swing rhythm. It is exactly the same as measures 3 and 4 of Example 1, but it appears as you would actually see it in most written music.

▶ **EXAMPLE 2 • 1:46**

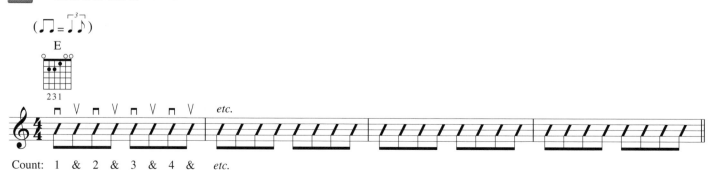

The next example also features **Strum Pattern 2**. Maintain a smooth and steady strum at a tempo that is comfortable for you.

EXAMPLE 3 · 2:06

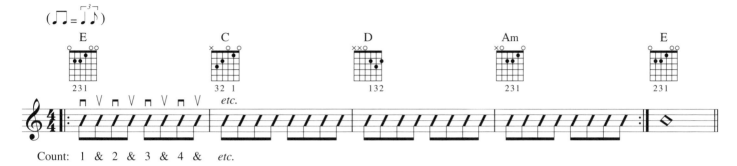

Count: 1 & 2 & 3 & 4 & *etc.*

STRUM PATTERN 3

Here's a great example using **Strum Pattern 3**. The swing rhythm is applied to the eighth notes on beats 2 and 4.

EXAMPLE 4 · 2:49

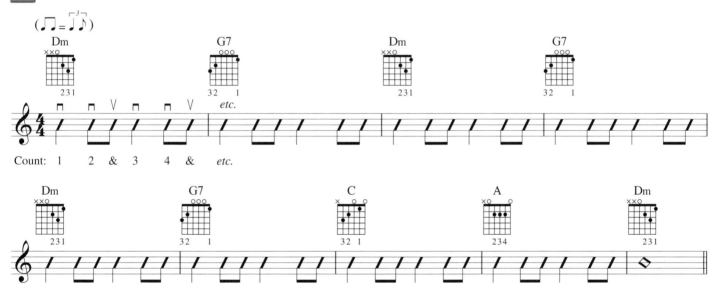

Count: 1   2 & 3   4 & *etc.*

STRUM PATTERN 4

The following example features **Strum Pattern 4**. The swing rhythm is applied to the eighth notes on beats 2, 3, and 4. A new voicing for A7 is included (see diagram to the right). To play this voicing, form the A chord that you already know with your first, second, and third fingers and then place your pinky on the third fret of the first string. This voicing sets up a cool descending line on the first string as you progress through the chords: third fret (G), second fret (F♯), first fret (F), and open string E.

EXAMPLE 5 · 3:42

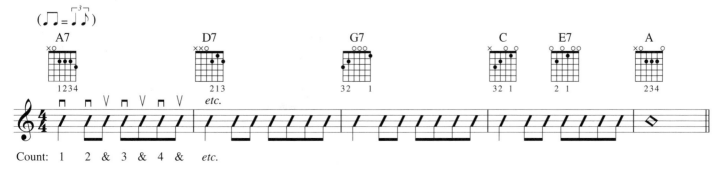

Count: 1   2 & 3 & 4 & *etc.*

STRUM PATTERN 5

Next, we have **Strum Pattern 5** played with a swing feel. The swing rhythm is applied to the eighth notes on beats 2, 3, and 4. This is tricky because, even though there is a tie from the "&" of beat 2 to the downbeat of beat 3, the swing feel must be maintained. So, make sure you are coming in at the right spot with the upstroke on the "&" of beat 3.

EXAMPLE 6 • 4:18

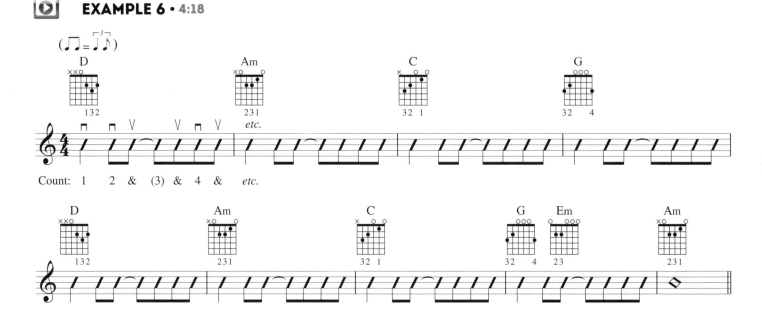

MIXING THE STRUMS AND STRUM-HAND MUTING

Next is "When Johnny Comes Marching Home," an American Civil War song from the early 1860s. This tune features **Strum Patterns 1, 3,** and **4**. **Strum Pattern 1** consists of quarter notes only, but you should still sense the swing feel in the context of the rest of the piece. As this tune should be played at a relatively brisk tempo, be sure to lift your fingers and start to place them in position on the eighth note *before* each chord change. This will ensure smooth transitions.

STRUM-HAND MUTING

It's time for a new technique. Notice the rapid chord changes on each quarter note in measures 1, 10, and 13. You can play these as strict quarter notes (letting each chord ring out for a full beat), or you can play them *staccato*, cutting them off before they ring out for their full value. The reasons for doing this are two-fold: 1) It has a cool percussive effect, 2) It allows you a bit more time to prepare for each new chord. Staccato is indicated with a dot above or below the note, and the sound of each staccato quarter note would almost be the same as an eighth note followed by an eighth *rest* (silence).

One way to achieve the staccato effect is with *strum-hand muting*. Immediately after strumming the chord, bring the side of your palm down on the strings to completely cut off the sound (see photo). Then, immediately get your hand in position to strum the next chord and repeat the process. Try measures 1, 10, and 13 with and without staccato. You can even alternate between staccato and no staccato within a single performance—this creates variety and interest.

Position of palm on strings for strum-hand muting

WHEN JOHNNY COMES MARCHING HOME

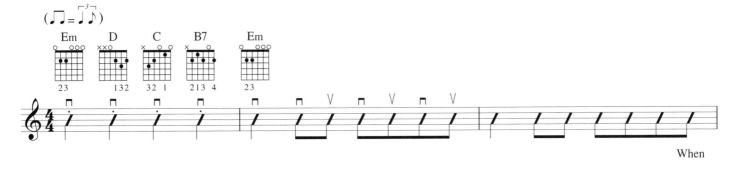

When

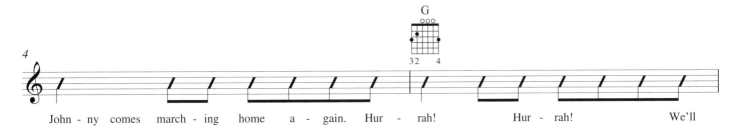

John - ny comes march - ing home a - gain. Hur - rah! Hur - rah! We'll

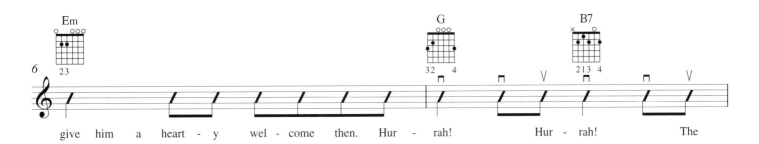

give him a heart - y wel - come then. Hur - rah! Hur - rah! The

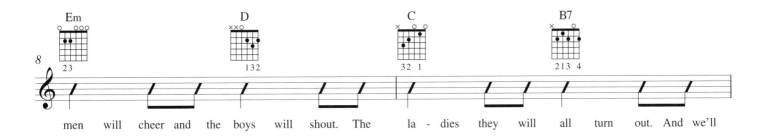

men will cheer and the boys will shout. The la - dies they will all turn out. And we'll

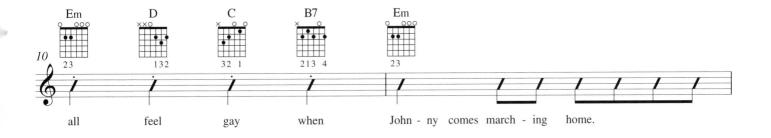

all feel gay when John - ny comes march - ing home.

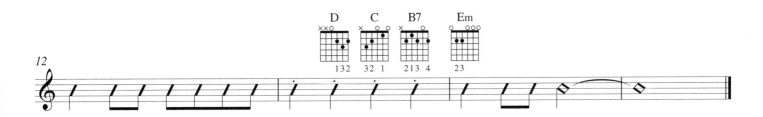

MORE BLUES

As mentioned on page 12, there are typically three chords in a 12-bar blues progression. The choice of chords depends on the key. Each key centers around a particular scale. For example, the key of C is based on the C major scale. There are seven tones in a major scale, and each tone is given a *scale degree*, or number:

C MAJOR SCALE

Scale Tone	C	D	E	F	G	A	B
Scale Degree	1	2	3	4	5	6	7

Chords can be built on top of each scale tone. In a major scale, the chord qualities would be: major–minor–minor–major–major–minor–diminished. Chords in a key are assigned Roman numerals (uppercase for major, and lowercase for minor and diminished). Below are the chords built on the C major scale—in other words, this is the *harmonized* C major scale.

C MAJOR SCALE HARMONIZED

Chord	C	Dm	Em	F	G	Am	B°
Roman Numeral	I	ii	iii	IV	V	vi	vii°

Notice that the I, IV, and V chord above are highlighted. These chords are known as the primary chords of the key, and these are the chords that appear in blues progressions and many other types of progressions and songs as well.

Let's look at the key of A:

A MAJOR SCALE

Scale Tone	A	B	C♯	D	E	F♯	G♯
Scale Degree	1	2	3	4	5	6	7

A MAJOR SCALE HARMONIZED

Chord	A	Bm	C♯m	D	E	F♯m	G♯°
Roman Numeral	I	ii	iii	IV	V	vi	vii°

In the key of A (the key of our next blues example), the I, IV, and V chords are A, D, and E. Dominant seventh chords are widely substituted for major chords in the blues, as is the case with "Swing Blues in A." Notice the Roman numerals above each chord in the progression.

Note that we go to the IV chord (D7) in measure 2—this is called a *quick four* or *quick change* because it returns to the I chord immediately in the following measure. In addition, check out the *turnaround* (the last four measures of a blues progression that set up the music to either repeat or end). In measures 11 and 12, there is a variation that changes quickly from I to IV to I to V. This creates anticipation to begin again or end on the I chord.

"Swing Blues in A" applies the swing rhythm to **Strum Pattern 5**, with the exception of measure 11, which uses **Strum Pattern 3**.

SWING BLUES IN A

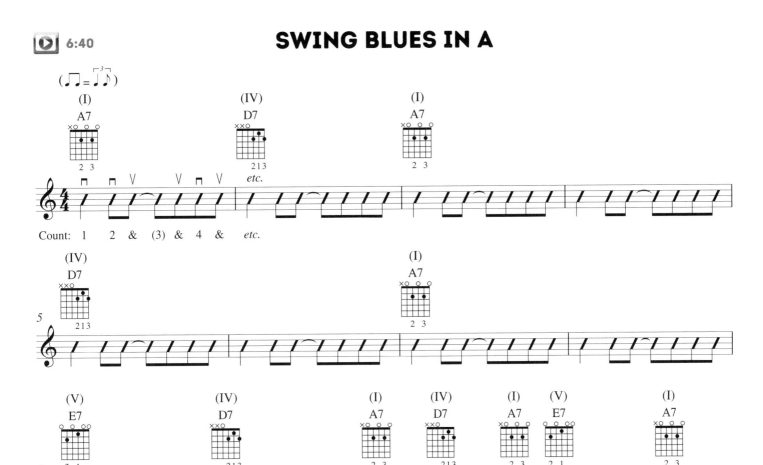

Our next example is a blues progression in the key of E.

E MAJOR SCALE

Scale Tone	E	F#	G#	A	B	C#	D#
Scale Degree	1	2	3	4	5	6	7

E MAJOR SCALE HARMONIZED

Scale Tone	E	F#m	G#m	A	B	C#m	D#o
Roman Numeral	I	ii	iii	IV	V	vi	viio

As you can see, our I, IV, and V chords are E, A, and B. Remember that we can substitute dominant sevenths for these as well. To create movement, in "Swing Blues in E," we quickly change between major chords, dominant seventh chords, and back to major chords on the same root. This produces a cool, bouncy feel, and it is not as difficult as it looks; for the E and E7 chords you are simply adding and taking away your pinky finger. The rhythm is a bit tricky because you are changing chords on the "&" of beats 2 and 3. Be sure to watch the video to get this right. Practice hard—it's worth it!

"Swing Blues in E" features **Strum Pattern 5** everywhere except for measures 9–10 (**Strum Pattern 2**) and measure 11 (**Strum Pattern 3**). Now, give this cool blues tune a try.

SWING BLUES IN E

CHAPTER 6
BASS STRUM AND ALTERNATING BASS

BASS STRUM

The *bass strum* is a technique that involves playing the bass note (the lowest note) of the chord first and then strumming the rest of the chord. The bass note is often the chord's root. For example, on a C chord, we would play the lowest note (C on the third fret of the fifth string, third finger) and then strum the rest of the chord. One approach is to play the bass note on the first beat of the measure and then strum the rest of the chord on the remaining quarter notes, as in Example 1 below. (Note: For this chapter, we will be using tab notation. For a review, see page 7.)

EXAMPLE 1 · 0:33

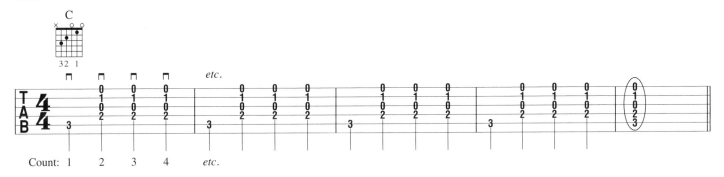

Another approach, which has a country feel, is to alternate the bass notes and chord strums every other beat, as with Example 2.

EXAMPLE 2 · 1:05

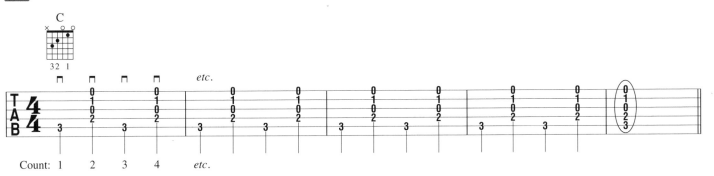

The following song, "Sussing the Bass," incorporates both of the above approaches: measures 1–8 are like Example 1, and measures 9–16 are like Example 2. This tune also has two suspended chords: Dsus2 (which you have already learned) and Asus2 (see diagram to the right). Asus2 is just like Am but without the first finger. Try this chord and then begin to master the bass-strum technique by practicing "Sussing the Bass."

SUSSING THE BASS

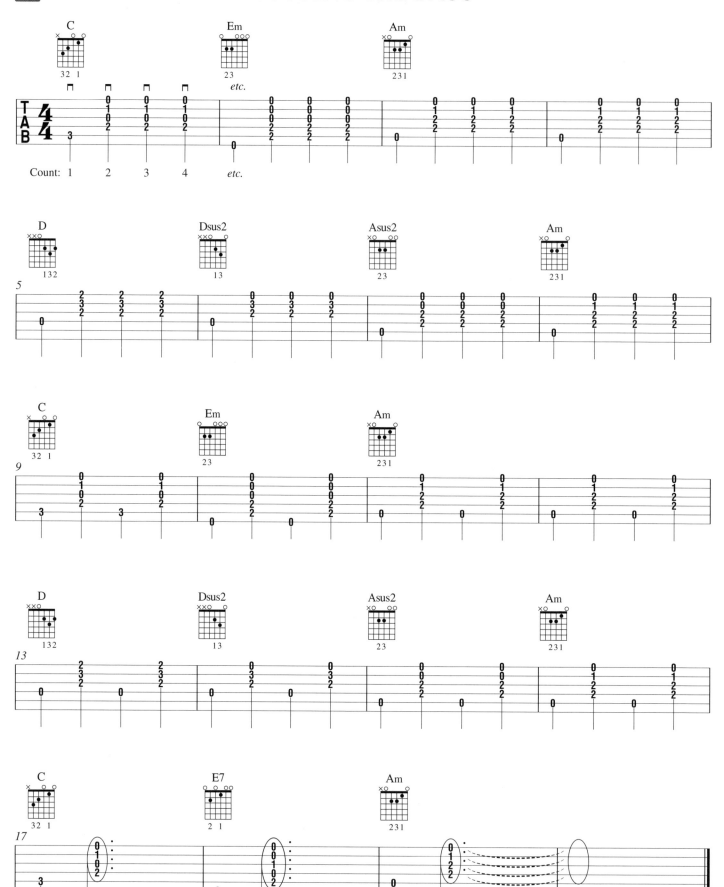

The following example uses our first approach to the bass strum and is in the style of "Rocky Raccoon" by the Beatles. It also features a new chord: Em7.

Em7

 3:04

THE MASKED PUGILIST

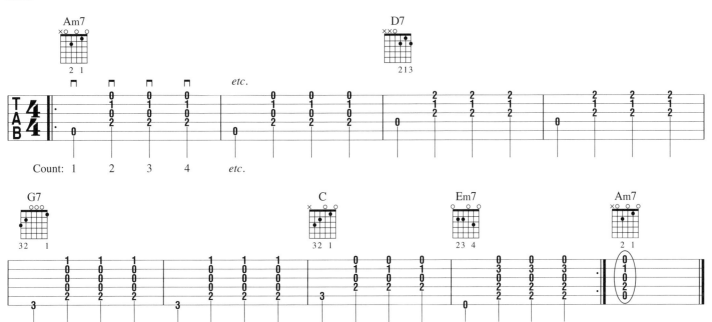

PLAYING IN 3/4 TIME AND THE HALF BARRE

Our next couple of examples are in 3/4 time, which means they have three beats per measure with the quarter note receiving the beat. In 3/4, the count is: 1, 2, 3, 1, 2, 3, etc. If a chord is supposed to ring out for a full measure, it is notated as a dotted half note, which equals three beats.

In 3/4, a typical bass-strum pattern would be: bass-strum-strum, bass-strum-strum. Check out the following example.

EXAMPLE 3 · 4:03

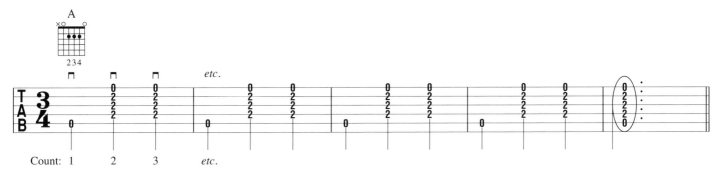

Our next couple of tunes also feature the F chord (see diagram to the right), which is played using the *barre* technique. A barre is the result of pressing a finger flat across two or more strings at the same fret and is indicated in chord diagrams by a curved line ⌒. The F chord requires you to fret the first and second strings at the first fret with the index finger. Lay the pad of your finger across these strings at the first fret and play each note separately to make sure they both ring clearly. Then add your second finger to the third string—curling it so as to fret the string with the fingertip. Check all the notes again and then add your third finger to the fourth string. Check all the notes and then strum the chord. It may be tricky to lay one finger flat

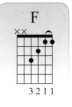
F

and curl the others in this manner, but with patience and practice, it will become second nature. When all six strings are barred (a technique not covered in this book), it is referred to as a *full barre*. When less than six strings are barred (as is the case with the F chord), it is referred to as a *half barre*, *partial barre*, or *small barre*.

Below are photos of the two-string barre and a fretted F chord.

Two-String Barre

Fretted F Chord

Our first song in this section is "Scarborough Fair," a traditional English ballad made famous through recordings by folk duo Simon & Garfunkel and many other artists. It is in 3/4, features the F chord, and includes a cool *vamp* (short, repeated phrase) on Dm that goes: Dsus2–Dm–Dsus2–Dm. This is accomplished by simply removing the first finger from the Dm chord and then placing it, removing it, etc. Play this song slowly at first, as there is a lot to work on here!

SCARBOROUGH FAIR

5:00

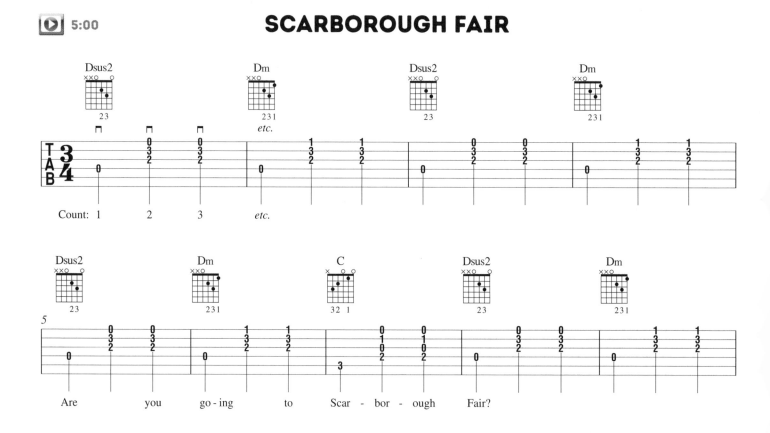

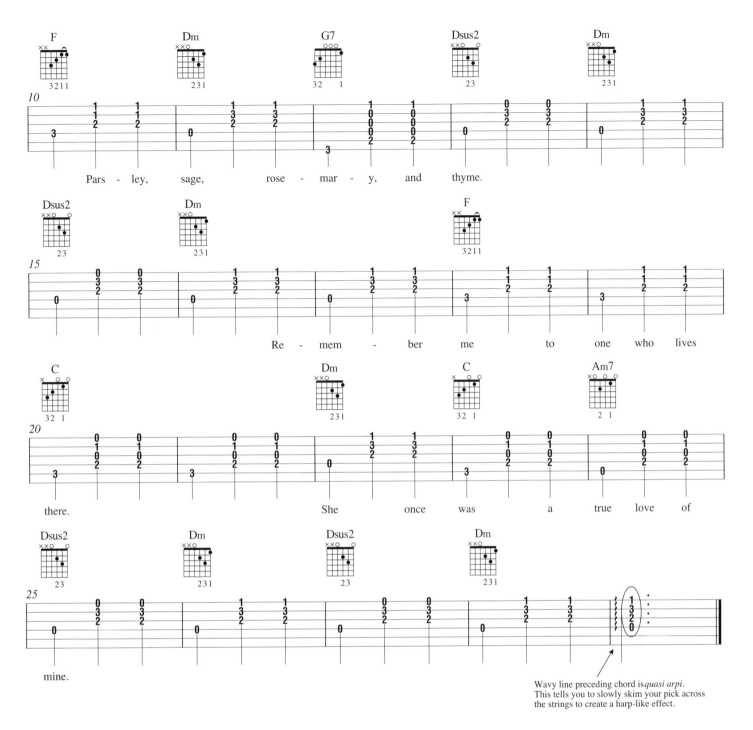

Pars - ley, sage, rose - mar - y, and thyme.

Re - mem - ber me to one who lives

there. She once was a true love of

mine.

Wavy line preceding chord is *quasi arpi*.
This tells you to slowly skim your pick across
the strings to create a harp-like effect.

Now, we're going to introduce eighth notes into the pattern. On beats 2 & 3 &, strum down-up, down-up, as demonstrated in the example below. Strum the eighth notes with a light touch, focusing on the top strings—it's not necessary to be too precise here; you don't have to hit all four strings on every strum. Sometimes, too much perfection can make you sound stiff. Loosen up and strive for a smooth, steady flow of notes and strums.

EXAMPLE 4 · 6:09

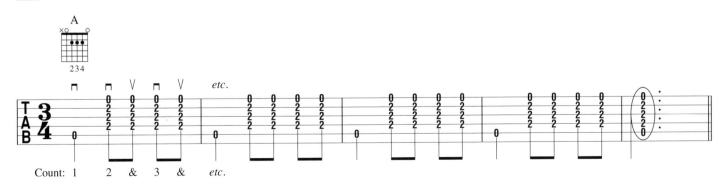

Our next tune is in the style of "You've Got to Hide Your Love Away" by the Beatles. It features the eighth-note bass strum and also single-note bass passages in measures 10 and 12. The purpose of these short bass runs is to provide momentum and lead into the new chords. Below these single notes, circled numbers tell you which fretting-hand fingers to use. Practice this one slowly at first and keep the strumming hand loose on those eighth notes.

STRUM YOUR EIGHTH NOTES AWAY

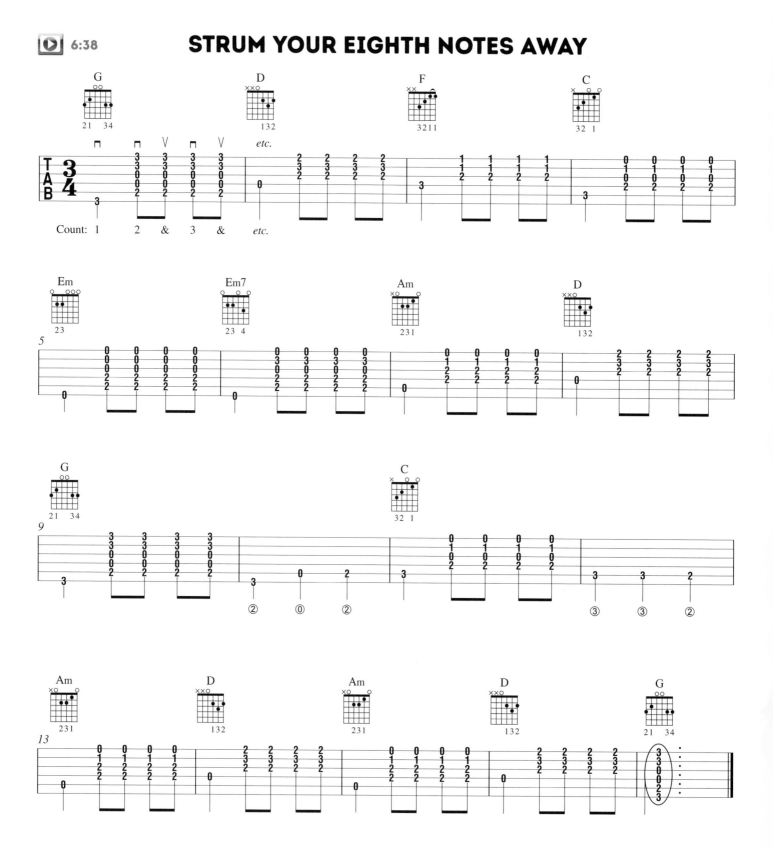

ALTERNATING BASS

Another bass-strum technique is known as alternating bass, where the root note alternates with another chord tone—usually the *5th* (five scale tones above the root). Sometimes, the alternating note is *below* the root, as in Example 5 below.

EXAMPLE 5 • 7:52

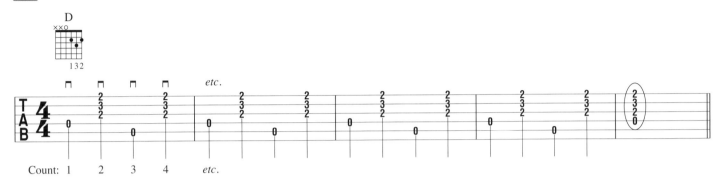

Sometimes, the alternating note is *above* the root, like Example 6.

EXAMPLE 6 • 8:43

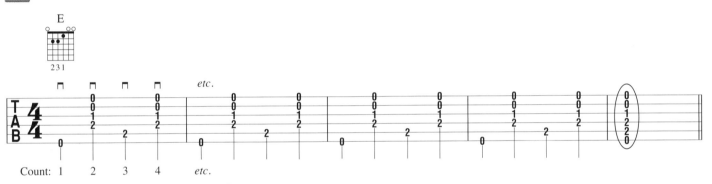

In Examples 5 and 6, the alternating notes were on open strings, but they can be fretted notes as well. For both the C and F chords, you have to remove your finger from the root note to place it on the alternating note and keep switching between the two. This may take some practice, but patience and dedication pay off. Don't get frustrated—even a few minutes a day on this will do wonders. You may find it useful at first to lightly anchor the side of your palm on the bridge when playing alternating bass. This can give your hand a frame of reference when alternating between different bass notes and chords.

EXAMPLE 7 • 9:41

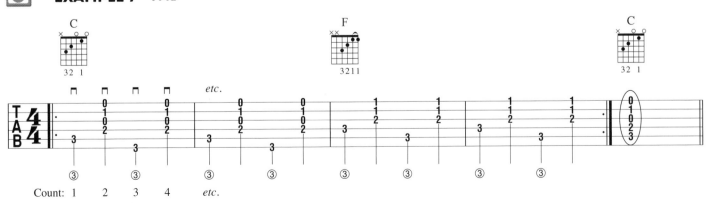

The following tune is in the style of "Ghost Riders in the Sky," a famous country song recorded by Johnny Cash, the Outlaws, and many others. It features the alternating bass style as well as single-note bass passages that produce a cool effect while leading into new chords. These passages can be found on beats 3 and 4 of measures 2, 6, 14, 16, etc. In addition, pay particular attention to the chord changes in measures 17–19 and 33–35, where the progression is F–Em–D. These chords change rapidly—especially considering the alternating bass—so practice these passages slowly. Also, note that the Em chord has you playing the root on the fourth string and alternating with the B note on the fifth string. This facilitates the descending bass line that occurs when changing between these chords. Now, enjoy playing "Ghosts on the Plains."

GHOSTS ON THE PLAINS

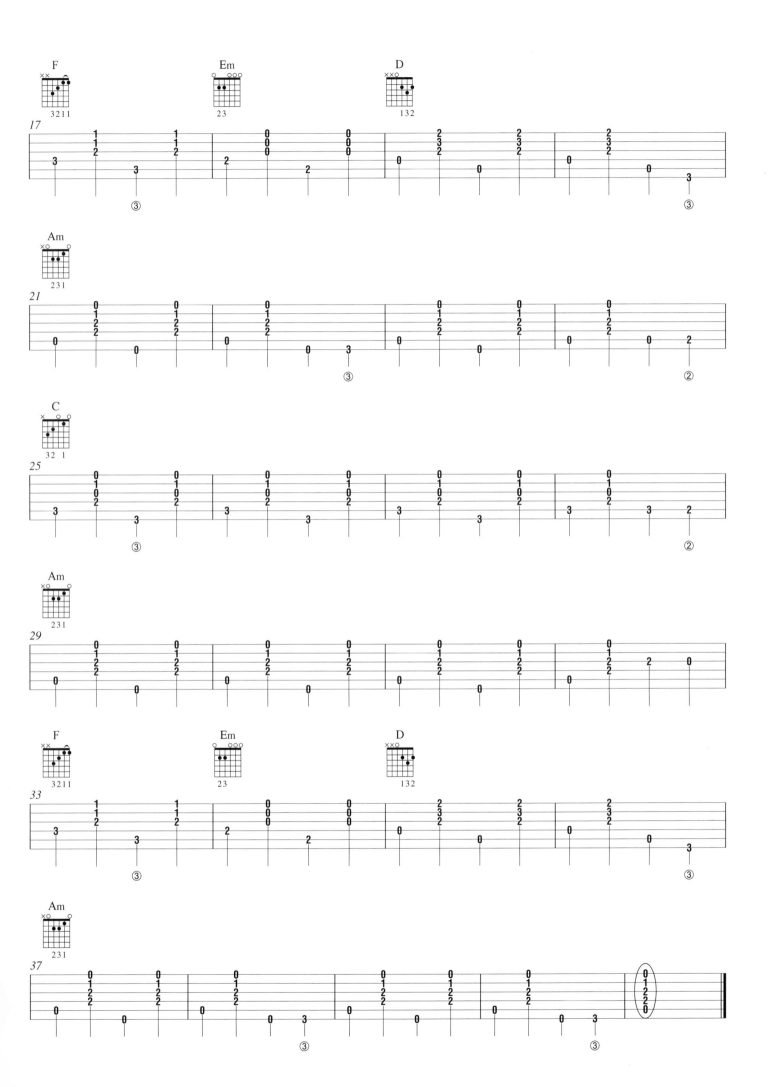

We'll conclude with a brief introduction to a couple of cool topics. The intention here is to whet your appetite, so you can look into these further or experiment on your own.

OPEN CHORD FORMS AROUND THE NECK

There are many open chord forms that sound great all over the fretboard. Just keep the fingering and move it to different frets, retaining the open strings from the original chord. *Slash chords* often result from this process. A slash chord consists of a chord name followed by a slash and another letter. The symbol to the left of the slash indicates the chord, and the letter to the right of the chord indicates the bass note. For instance, F/D is the symbol for an F major chord with a D note in the bass (called "F over D").

In Example 1, we are playing a D chord and then moving the fingering to the fifth fret, seventh fret, second fret, third fret, and back to the second fret. Jimmy Page uses this technique on many Led Zeppelin tunes. (Note: When chords move outside of the open position, fret numbers are shown to the right of the fretboard.)

▶ **EXAMPLE 1 · 0:58**

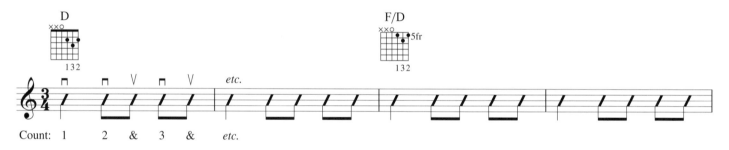

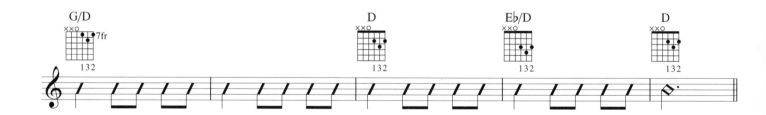

Here's another example based on the fingerings for the E and Fmaj7 chord forms.

EXAMPLE 2 • 1:46

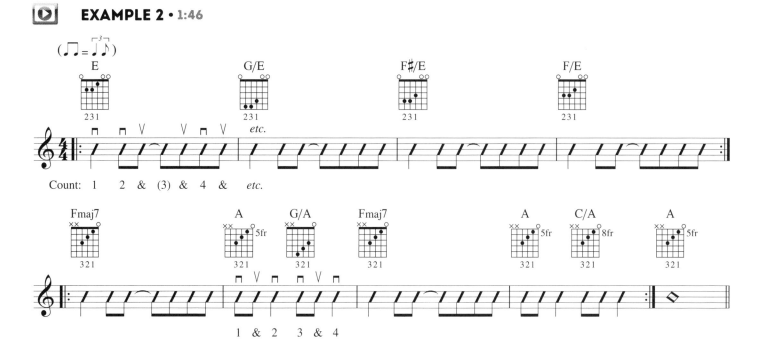

INTRODUCTION TO FUNK STRUMMING

Syncopated 16th-note strumming patterns are key to the funk guitar style. Remember: It takes four 16th notes to equal a beat, and they are counted: 1-e-&-ah, 2-e-&-ah, etc. Syncopation is the emphasis of "off beats" or upbeats—parts of a measure that aren't usually emphasized. For instance, in the next example, you are strumming the chord on the "ah" of beats 2 and 3. "Chucking," or fret-hand muting, facilitates syncopation while adding a cool percussive effect. When you see an "X" note head, lift your fingers from the chord just enough to deaden the sound, so that they are resting on the strings without being lifted off completely. When this form is strummed, the result should be an unpitched, percussive sound (see photo below). It will take some practice to press and release your fingers at the right times, so work on this very slowly at first. Your right hand should alternate downstrums and upstrums in a constant 16th-note rhythm. Try Example 3, which also introduces the A13 chord (see diagram to the right). (Note: The root note in A13 may ring out even when you are chucking, but don't worry about that right now.)

Release finger pressure when chucking

EXAMPLE 3 • 3:33

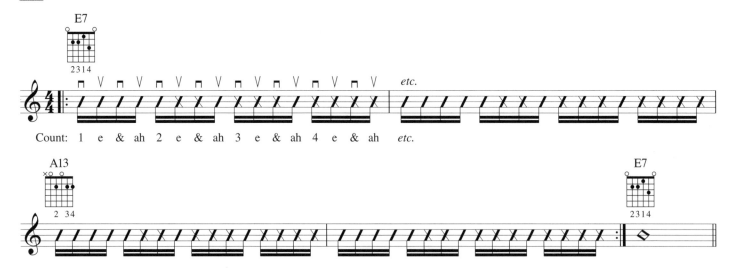

Count: 1   e   &   ah   2   e   &   ah   3   e   &   ah   4   e   &   ah   *etc.*

Below is another strumming pattern that features a very funky chord: the 7♯9. You've had some experience moving around the neck in the previous section, so we'll have you move from the second fret to the seventh fret in this example. Check out the chords to the right and then give this one a shot. Remember, figure out the rhythm and play it slowly at first. Use the counting numbers and letters to help you get it right.

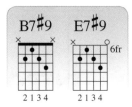

EXAMPLE 4 • 5:31

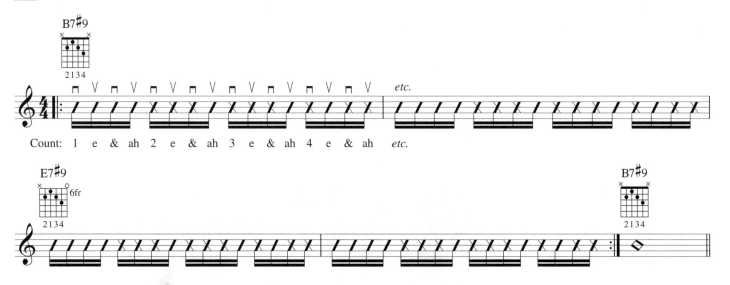

Count: 1   e   &   ah   2   e   &   ah   3   e   &   ah   4   e   &   ah   *etc.*

Congratulations! You have made it to the end of this book and have a firm grasp of various strumming styles and techniques. To continue your studies, check out some other great Hal Leonard books like *Easy Pop Rhythms* and *The Guitar Three-Chord Songbook*. Most important is that you have fun. Strum along with friends, musicians, and singers—all of whom can teach you so much. Enjoy!